Gypsy Traveller Students in Secondary Schools
culture, identity and achievement

Gypsy Traveller Students in Secondary Schools
culture, identity and achievement

Chris Derrington and Sally Kendall

Trentham Books
Stoke on Trent, UK and Sterling, USA

Trentham Books Limited

Westview House	22883 Quicksilver Drive
734 London Road	Sterling
Oakhill	VA 20166-2012
Stoke on Trent	USA
Staffordshire	
England ST4 5NP	

First published 2004

British Library Cataloguing-in-Publication Data
A catalogue record for this book is available from the British Library

1 85856 320 8

Designed and typeset by Trentham Print Design Ltd., Chester and printed in Great Britain by Cromwell Press Ltd, Wiltshire.

Contents

Acknowledgements

The authors would like to thank all the Traveller students and their families who contributed to the study over the course of the three years. Their willingness to be involved and talk about their experiences are the key to this book and their insights brought these issues to life in a way which otherwise would not have been possible.

We are also grateful to all the Traveller Education Services and the school staff who took part in the project and gave up their time to be interviewed. We would also like to thank the advisory group: Peter Mercer, Arthur Ivatts, Thomas Acton, Brian Foster, Terry Suddaby, Alan Roach, Alison Venner-Jones and Jenny Robson for the time they gave to the project, their words of advice and encouragement and for reading and commenting on the draft manuscript.

Finally, thanks to Gillian Klein and to our colleagues at the NFER and University College Northampton for their valued support and contributions: Anne Wilkin, Kay Kinder, Richard Rose, Vicky Bland, Ann Black, Hilary McElderry and Julie Thompson.

Foreword
Culture, identity and achievement

Life isn't easy for a Travelling family, especially those with school children, for one reason: the desire to move. School can put pressure on a lot of Travelling children because of bullying. My name is Tammy, I am fourteen years old and school is easy for me, I am accepted for what I am. I would like people to learn that our culture is important and that we respect their culture as much as they should respect ours. It is important for Travellers to go to secondary school to get a chance to have as much as everyone else. It is important that Travellers express their views along with other people and stand up and be heard so that they don't feel like outcasts. I think schools should have citizenship lessons so that Travelling children can show other children what their lives are really like. My hopes and dreams are that one day the Travelling culture will be accepted.

Although I want to have a good career, I know that some day I will be travelling with my horses through a shady back road ready to stay in a flower-laden meadow.

They move along

They move along everyday
Because it was the only way
The horses, the wagons, the carts and bikes too
People knew when they were on the move.
At night there was a fire
I remember my father fixing a tyre
The horses on tethers
The goldfinches with neat feathers
For years and years
They lived that way
And, as far as I know
They're still travelling today
By Tammy Loveridge (age 14)

1
Introduction

This book presents and discusses the data and definitive findings from the first national longitudinal study of Gypsy Traveller students in English secondary schools. The focus of this unique phenomenological study, which was sponsored by the Nuffield Foundation between February 2000 and December 2003, was the educational experiences of 44 Gypsy Traveller children (from different parts of England) as they prepared for secondary transfer and progressed through Key Stage 3.[1] The students who took part in this research were predominantly English Gypsy Travellers, although six of the students were Travellers of Irish descent. The term 'Gypsy Traveller' is adopted to encompass both groups and is used to differentiate between English Gypsy/Irish Travellers on the one hand and Fairground/Circus or New Age Travellers on the other. (The term 'Traveller' is used throughout the text for convenience and is not intended to cause offence or misrepresentation).[2]

Through prolonged engagement with the students concerned, as well as with their parents and teachers over the three-year period, the authors collected and analysed a wealth of data relating to attitudes, values, expectations, aspirations, experiences and achievement. The research therefore provides not only a longitudinal account but also a wider, multi-perspective dimension from which the authors identify typologies and associations that may support and encourage Traveller students to engage and achieve in Key Stage 3. The research project was managed by the National Foundation for Educational Research (NFER) and was endorsed and supported throughout by an Advisory Group that included representatives from Traveller organisations, the Department for Education and Skills, Ofsted, secondary schools, Traveller Education Services and Higher Education. The research involved a total of fifteen Local Education Authorities representing the South East, East Anglia, the East Midlands and the North of England. All the children in the study and their parents agreed to take part in the three-year study.

Background literature and historical overview

Historically, Gypsy Travellers have been universally stigmatised and treated with hostility by the majority culture. When the first Gypsies arrived in the UK in the fifteenth century, they were treated with suspicion by both the Church and the State. Under the reign of Henry VIII, Gypsies were outlawed and in 1562, Elizabeth I made it a capital offence to be a Gypsy. Within a climate of social, political and religious flux, Gypsies became the near perfect scapegoat and, by the end of the sixteenth century, there was widespread intolerance towards them across Europe (Ivatts, 2003). Therefore it is perhaps unsurprising that almost every European country has, at some time, outlawed their nomadic way of life. During the second world war, an estimated half a million Gypsies were annihilated by the Nazi regime, although these acts of genocide were never addressed at the Nuremberg trials and have been repressed and obscured ever since (Bedford and Rawcliffe, 1999). In more recent years, Gypsies continue to be perceived as a 'problem' by the settled community. Not only do Gypsy Travellers have to contend with inherently racist attitudes at the individual level, they are also subjected to a degree of legal and institutional racism unprecedented in any other minority ethnic group, despite being ostensibly protected by Race Relations legislation (Derrington and Thorp, 1990). Urbanisation and planning legislation has led to a severe shortage of legal stopping places and in 1994, the Criminal Justice and Public Order Act repealed the duty on local authorities to provide sufficient authorised sites for Travellers in their area. This effectively criminalised the traditional Traveller way of life and heightened tensions between the Traveller and settled communities. An estimated one in five Travellers has no legal or secure place to stay (DfES 2003).

Traveller Education

The Plowden Report *Children and their Primary Schools* (DES, 1967) described Gypsy children as 'probably the most severely deprived children in the country' and concluded that most Gypsy children did not access school and their needs were 'largely unmet'. Reiss (1975) reported on a Schools' Council Project on the education of Traveller children and recommended urgent action to address Traveller children's access to and attendance at school. In the same year, Ivatts (1975) examined the secondary school experiences of housed Travellers and identified negative attitudes and inflexible approaches in the schools and poor attendance and attainment amongst Traveller students. A discussion paper *The Education of Travellers' Children* (HMI, 1983) reiterated these concerns regarding the underachievement and poor attendance of Traveller students.

Nearly twenty years after the Plowden Report, the Swann Report (DES, 1985), showed that little had changed. This report was published as a result of a government inquiry into the education of children from ethnic minorities. Although originally established to investigate underachievement amongst African-Caribbean students, it acknowledged that:

> In many ways the situation of travellers' (sic) children in Britain today throws into stark relief many of the factors which influence the education of children from other ethnic minority groups – racism and discrimination, myths and stereotyping and misinformation, the inappropriateness of the education system. (DES, 1985).

In 1989 Hyman highlighted the vulnerability of Traveller students within the education system and access to secondary education was seen as a particular issue of concern. In the 1990s developments affecting the education of Traveller children accelerated, largely due to the introduction of a centralised funding arrangement in 1990, which replaced the No Area Pool.[3] This arrangement gave Local Educational Authorities the opportunity to bid for a specific grant aimed at 'ensuring unhindered access to, and full integration [of Traveller children] in mainstream education' (DES, 1990). This funding was earmarked for 'extra' expenditure and provision above and beyond the support that should be made available for all students, including Travellers. The result was the development and increase in dedicated Traveller Education Services (TESs) employing co-ordinators, peripatetic teachers, classroom assistants and welfare officers (Ofsted, 1996). Increasing numbers of Traveller students were registered in the primary phase but 'access to school for secondary aged children remains a matter of grave concern' (Ofsted, 1996). It was estimated that only 15 to 20 per cent of secondary age Traveller children were enrolled at schools in England, with up to 10,000 young Travellers not even registered. Of those who did transfer to the secondary phase, a disproportionate number were excluded from school, 'despite the general assessment that the behaviour of Traveller pupils is good'. Other, comparative studies highlighted similar findings across Europe (Liegeois, 1998) and in relation to Irish Travellers in the USA (Andereck, 1992).

Recent studies of attitudes and actions that may affect the engagement of Gypsy Traveller children have included those by Clay (1999), Jordan (1996; 2001), Kiddle (1999) and Lloyd et al (1999). Although it should be emphasised that Travellers do not constitute a single homogenous group, a number of common and significant cultural influences have been identified in the literature concerning non-participation at secondary school. Adolescence is traditionally the time when young Travellers are expected to help generate income or take on a wider range of domestic responsibilities. Some parents may hold the belief that secondary education has little value or relevance to the Traveller lifestyle. Many Traveller parents express anxieties about their children's moral, emotional and physical welfare in what they perceive to be a strange and hostile environment. A survey in Sheffield found that 'racist name- calling was the thing Traveller children most hated about going to school' (Kenrick and Bakewell, 1995). Similarly, Lloyd et al's (1999) study of Travellers in Scottish secondary schools found that conflict with teachers often led to non-attendance and that much of what schools saw as a lack of discipline in the form of violent behaviour, for example, may have been in response to racist name-calling.

Department for Education and Employment statistics for the periods 1996-97 and 1997-98 revealed a further decline in the number of secondary age Traveller students enrolled at school, although primary enrolments were on the increase (DfEE, 1998, 1999). The

Ofsted report, *Raising the Attainment of Minority Ethnic Pupils* (Ofsted, 1999) found that Gypsy Travellers were 'the group most at risk in the education system' and that attainment in secondary school was a matter of serious concern. In half of the schools surveyed, no Gypsy Traveller child had ever taken a GCSE exam, and many had opted out of education by the end of Key Stage 3. Bhopal *et al*'s (2000) study for the DfEE *Working towards inclusive education* again addressed the issue of low attainment amongst Traveller students and identified effective practice in improving attendance and raising attainment. The report highlighted the need for higher expectations of Traveller pupils, the need for effective anti-bullying policies and the importance of the role of the TES in terms of helping Traveller students' access and achievement within the secondary school context. In 2003, the DfES published a good practice guide that offered advice and guidance in improving the attendance and achievement of Traveller pupils (DfES 2003). The report acknowledged that there was 'still a long way to go ... for the secondary age group in particular'.

This brief overview of the literature shows that, whilst there have been some notable developments since Plowden (1967) concerning Traveller students' access to school, serious issues regarding their attendance and attainment, particularly at the secondary phase, remain. Recent studies, such as Bhopal *et al* (2000) and DfES (2003) have begun to highlight elements of good practice in Traveller education but the current research is the first longitudinal study of a group of Traveller students exploring their educational experiences as they approach and advance through Key Stage 3. It is unique in that it presents the perspectives and insights from Traveller students, their parents, TES and school staff. It is hoped that these perspectives will contribute to and develop the existing body of research in this area.

Aims of the research

The purpose of the research was to investigate the complex issue of secondary school attendance for Traveller children and to gain a clearer insight into the nature of the difficulties that have been identified by researchers and policy makers over the past forty years or so (Bhopal, 2000). As Rose and Shevlin (2003) point out, research about children is most meaningful when the children themselves are given the opportunity to articulate their own views, ideas and perceptions. Therefore, the primary intention of this study was to enable Traveller students themselves to broaden our insight into the complexity of issues surrounding their continued engagement in school beyond the age of 11. Essentially, this was to be a phenomenological study that aimed to explore the students' experiences and perceptions of secondary school. The second intention was to capture a holistic view by involving significant others (the students' parents and teachers) in order to identify patterns and relationships of meaning. The stated aims of the research proposal were to:

- Map and record the educational progress, engagement and experiences of a sample of 50 Gypsy Traveller students over a three-year period as they approach and advance through Key Stage 3

- Gather and report upon the personal reflections, accounts, expectations and aspirations of the students, their families and teachers

- Identify and examine a range of factors which may affect attitudes, levels of achievement and continued involvement in secondary education

- Identify associations and typologies which support and encourage Gypsy Traveller students to transfer successfully to secondary school and continue to engage in formal education

- Inform teachers and policy makers of the findings, highlight good practice, promote discussion and identify areas for further research and development.

Methodology and research design

The research employed a qualitative paradigm and a phenomenological design, as described by Creswell (1994). In this design human experiences are examined through prolonged engagement with the subject(s) with the aim of addressing the question 'What is it like for ...?' (In this case Traveller students in secondary school) (Nieswiadomy, 1993). Our longitudinal study spanned a three-year period.

The authors' contribution to the research setting

One of the researchers had formerly managed a LEA Traveller Education Service and had several years' experience of teaching Traveller students in school. The other had previously been involved in community work with Traveller children and women, including adult literacy programmes. This background was important in that it facilitated contact with gatekeepers such as TES teams and perhaps brought a level of contextual knowledge, sensitivity and understanding that helped to establish good relationships with the participants. Both researchers were female, which may have been beneficial when interviewing mothers in their homes.

Biases brought to the study

Although all efforts were made to ensure objectivity, the fact that the researchers were not Travellers was bound to influence the responses of the students and their parents. Despite the fact that interviews were conducted in an informal manner, and the consistency of the researcher/participant relationship over the three-year period, it is likely that some of the responses were influenced by the unnatural experience of being interviewed by a *gauje*[4] involved in education. Similarly, multiple realities exist in all qualitative studies and despite all efforts to maximise an objective interpretation of the data, this will almost certainly have been influenced by the researchers' inability to 'get inside' the participants' life-world and, in particular, the Traveller culture. Where possible, the voices of the participants have been reported verbatim.

Ethical considerations

By its very nature, ethnographic research is obtrusive and sensitive information is revealed. No school or LEA is named in the research and pseudonyms are used for the students. Quotations and references that contain sensitive information are not attributed directly.

Data Collection

The sample

The original aim was to study a total of 50 students. In the event, 44 students and their parents agreed to participate. Initial contact and subsequent access to students and their families were facilitated through the use of gatekeepers. Eight TES co-ordinators from one region of the country were the first point of contact. These co-ordinators were convened in the early stages of the project to act as a focus group. From there, the co-ordinators asked their team members to identify and approach parents and children in their final year of primary school in order to draw up the sample. Some difficulties emerged during this phase as three of the LEAs that had a mix of primary and middle schools in their areas had problems in identifying Traveller students. In other cases, parents were unwilling to become involved. Therefore we decided to approach five additional TES co-ordinators in adjoining authorities to the north and south, in order to recruit more participants.

The main criterion for selection was that of being relatively settled in the educational sense. In other words, all students in the study had been regularly engaged in primary school education for at least the preceding two years. Although this effectively excluded highly mobile groups, the justification for this criterion was that it would help to distinguish factors associated with secondary school engagement as opposed to access to schooling per se. In order to obtain a mix of students, additional criteria for selection included variables such as gender, type of living accommodation, siblings' experiences of secondary school, ability and parental attitudes.

The final sample therefore comprised 24 boys and 20 girls of whom:

- twenty-one lived on authorised local authority owned Traveller sites

- twelve lived in housing

- eight lived on authorised privately owned (or rented) plots

- three lived on unauthorised sites (including roadside encampments).

Other participants included parents (mostly mothers); older siblings and other adult relatives; primary school headteachers; Year 6 class teachers; heads of year in secondary schools; headteachers and deputy heads in secondary schools; special needs co-ordinators (SENCOs) in the case of students with special educational needs;

form tutors and TES teachers and/or TES fieldworkers. Additional interviews were held with learning support assistants (2) and in the case of two other students, whose parents had opted for Education Otherwise,[5] interviews were conducted with their private tutors. Directors of Education (in each of the LEAs involved) were contacted by letter at the outset of the project and all gave permission for the research to be conducted. Colleagues in Traveller Education Services supplied the names of the primary and secondary schools and these were subsequently contacted directly by the researchers and supplied with full details of the research project.

Methods

Data were collected each April and November throughout the three-year period. This was to avoid the traditional travelling patterns, to which some Traveller families are known to adhere during the summer months. There were three rounds of face-to-face interviews with all groups of participants listed above. These took place in the summer term of Year 6, the autumn term in Year 8 and the spring term of Year 9. In a small minority of cases, telephone interviews were held with professionals if visits were difficult to arrange. The authors conducted the interviews (with some additional support from another experienced NFER researcher during the latter stages). Semi-structured interview schedules were designed and discussed with the Advisory Group at each stage of the research. The schedules were based around a framework of common themes (Appendix 1) that was designed to elicit a multi-perspective account and to triangulate accounts of events. Each interview lasted around 45 minutes to one hour although some were considerably longer. Because the interviews were semi-structured and open ended, a rich set of qualitative data could be accrued. However, it should be noted that not all participants chose to speak about the same issues in the same amount of depth and this has obvious implications for analysis. For example, the counting of responses is not always possible or appropriate in an ideographic study such as this.

Interviews with teachers and headteachers were held in schools, interviews with TES staff took place in either schools or TES offices and interviews with the students and their parents were usually conducted in their own homes, although some of the students were interviewed in school. All interviews were pre-arranged. Electrical recording equipment was not used in the first round with Traveller respondents as the authors thought this approach might be daunting for the participants. On the suggestion of the Advisory Group, permission to be tape-recorded was sought and granted for the other rounds and this approach was felt to be successful. All taped interviews were transcribed. Other sources such as school policy documents, student progress reports, attendance print outs and national data such as school performance tables and Ofsted[6] reports were also used as part of the analysis process. This triangulation strengthens reliability as well as internal validity (Merrium, 1988).

Between the three rounds of interviews, additional interim data were collected via the use of short proformas to schools and TES's. These were sent out at the beginning of Year 7 and at the end of Year 8 and sought a combination of qualitative data as well as some quantitative information such as attendance figures, confirmation of SATs[7] results and numbers of Traveller students in each year group. TES personnel carried out informal interviews with students and parents as part of their usual monitoring role and recorded their perceptions on the form.

Finally, schools were asked to supply the research team with copies of relevant school policy documents such as attendance, behaviour and race equality. Not every school was able to supply these.

Analysis

Because of the vast amount of data collected over the course of the study (including well over four hundred interview transcripts as well as the questionnaires) the data were inputted into the Winmax data analysis software programme using a system of coding that was initially based on the thematic framework. As each transcript was imported into the programme and coded in segments, more superordinate themes were identified and added. The inputting of data was time consuming but the software facilitated a more efficient means of sorting and retrieving the data. The data were analysed using an approach that was informed by interpretative phenomenological analysis (IPA). This has been described by Smith and Osborn (2003) as the attempt to unravel meaning through an interpretative engagement with the transcripts and the identification of themes and clusters within and across cases.

Reporting the findings

The book provides a descriptive and narrative account of the findings. As with most qualitative research, data are reported in words rather than in numbers. In keeping with phenomenological research methods, an ideographic approach is used whereby the data are predominantly interpreted in relation to the particulars of individual cases rather than attempting to make generalisations (Creswell, 1994). The words of the participants are written throughout in embedded quotes as well as longer extracts. The children have been given pseudonyms and none of the teachers or schools are named. Particularly sensitive information is reported in a way that further protects anonymity. Some data are presented in tabular form where a comparison of responses is useful. Each chapter is concluded with a number of 'points for reflection'. The purpose of this is to stimulate debate and discussion that may help to move the agenda forward.

The book is divided into nine chapters. The first sets the context of the empirical research by providing a synthesis of existing knowledge, an overview of the relevant literature and a description of the research aims and methods.

Chapter 2 describes the experiences and processes that led up to the children's transfer from primary school to secondary school. It gives an overview of the primary schools in the study, examines the expectations of teachers, students and parents and explores policy and practice for effective transition. This chapter concludes with a description of the experiences of three children who failed to transfer to secondary school and analyses the significant factors.

In Chapter 3, the focus is shifted to the secondary schools in the study. This chapter investigates how attitudes, policies and practices within these institutions may support or discourage the retention of Traveller students. One headteacher who was interviewed used the metaphor of 'oak trees' and 'willow trees' to differentiate between rigid and flexible responses. This model is developed and illustrated using examples from the data.

Chapter 4 examines and analyses the role of LEA Traveller Education Services (referred to throughout as TESs). It highlights the variation in terms of policy and practice, discusses the extent to which TES impact on the continued engagement of Traveller students in secondary schools and describes some of the tensions that can exist as a result of conflicting expectations and loyalties.

In Chapter 5, the discussion and analysis is focused on concepts of cultural identity and cultural dissonance. This chapter explores how conflicting value and belief systems may impact on school retention. Students' perceptions of their cultural identity are analysed, including the extent to which they identified with social and cultural practices of their own, as well as the majority culture in school.

Chapter 6 describes the students' perceptions and experiences of racism in school. It examines the nature and prevalence of racial bullying and harassment and the way in which students, parents and teachers responded. The coping strategies that students adopt are examined and school policies for monitoring and dealing with racial harassment are considered.

The following two chapters both provide cross case comparisons by using student portraits (mini case studies) to explore the variables and common factors that may be associated with retention in secondary school. Chapter 7 looks specifically at the experiences of four students who left school before the end of Key Stage 3 and compares their experience with other students who left school during the course of the research. Chapter 8 focuses on the experiences of four students who successfully completed Key Stage 3 and analyses whether any factors are exclusive to other 'retained' students.

Finally, Chapter 9 presents a discussion of the implications drawn out in the preceding chapters and includes a section on student attainment. The book concludes with a summary of the main findings from this research.

Notes

1 Key Stage 3 refers to the period of secondary education for students between the ages of 11 and 14 years.

2 See McCann *et al.*, (1994), Acton, (1979) and (1985) for extended discussion of Traveller group identities

3 Prior to 1990, the No Area Pool was a source of finance available to support the education of children who did not 'belong' to a particular area. Although 75% of teacher costs could be reclaimed, many education authorities chose not to, through a lack of political will.

4 A Romani term to describe a non-Traveller.

5 Education Otherwise refers to the entitlement of parents to make their own arrangements for the education of their children at home.

6 Office for Standards in Education

7 Standardised Attainment Tests set nationally at ages 7, 11 and 14

2

Moving from primary to secondary

The point of transfer from primary to secondary school is recognised as a potential source of anxiety for many students (Measor and Woods, 1984; Delamont, 1991). For Traveller students whose families may have had virtually no experience of the secondary school environment, along with cultural concerns regarding the negative influences of a secondary education and the possibility of racial bullying, the prospect of transfer can be fraught with even greater anxiety. For students the transition from primary to secondary school can also be seen as reflecting a transition from childhood to adolescence, a 'rite of passage' (Glaser and Strauss, 1967), marking a change in status and identity (Measor and Woods, 1984), something which Traveller parents might have particular concerns about.

Gross and Burdett (1996) acknowledge that the 'potentially stressful nature of school transfer at 11 is well recognised by schools and most have developed policies and liaison practices to ease the process. They suggest that group discussions or external counselling with someone from outside school, in addition to school-based activities, might also assist in reducing students' stress about transfer. Hardy (1988) highlights the benefits of slowly developing links with students and their parents through shared teaching and site use, mutual profiling and assessment techniques, so that parents are already familiar with the school and the staff when students transfer. In addition, a practice of home visiting was used by the secondary school in order to develop and strengthen home/school liaison once students had transferred.

Hence considerable literature exists regarding the possible concerns and issues associated with secondary transfer. Against this context, this chapter considers the experiences and issues relating to secondary transfer arising for Traveller students and their parents. It begins with an overview of the primary schools in the study and goes on to examine expectations of transfer, methods of support for parents and students, issues of parental choice and the quality of the relationship between primary and secondary schools. It concludes by providing three case studies of students who did not transfer and some points for reflection on transfer and retention.

The primary schools in the study

The 44 students in the study attended 33 primary schools in 13 LEAs. The majority (21) of the schools were in urban locations, equally divided between cities and towns, whilst the remaining 12 students were attending village schools in rural locations. The size of the schools varied from a two-class primary with only 48 students to a large school with just under 400 students, although most of the children attended medium sized primary schools with an average of 261 students per school.

The proportion of Traveller students within the primary schools varied from 0.3 per cent to 20-30 per cent of the school population, which may have affected issues of identity, cultural awareness and support. Nearly a quarter of the sample attended primary schools where they and their siblings or cousins were the only Traveller students in the school. In the case of three children in the study, they were the only Travellers in their school. This cultural isolation of Traveller students increased within the secondary phase as their numbers decreased. In terms of absolute numbers the school with the largest number of Traveller students (40 to 60) was also the one with the largest proportion of Travellers. The actual numbers of Traveller students may have been greater as these were only the students identified by schools as Travellers and some children may have hidden their identity (see Chapter 5).

Nearly half (15) of the schools had some previous experience of Traveller students because there was an established local authority or private site nearby. A number of schools said Traveller students had attended over the past ten or fifteen years and there were a few schools where students' parents and in one instance grandparents had attended as a child. This included Gemma's family who were living on the roadside and whose mother had attended the same primary school as her daughter. However, in a number of instances students were not living in the catchment area but parents had chosen the school specifically because it was seen as having a good reputation with Traveller students, which shows the importance of developing trusting relationships with parents.

Eight of the schools had little or no history of admitting Travellers and in a few instances Traveller students in the study were believed to be the first in the school. Louis, Kizzie, Seamus and Matthew's families had to go to appeal before their children were admitted, and, in the case of Louis and Seamus, hostility from non-Traveller parents and the school meant that they 'fought long and hard to stop them coming in' (primary headteacher). Other headteachers described hostility within the local community and acknowledged this to be a significant factor in Traveller students' experiences at school.

Table 2.1 shows that just over half (17) the sample had attended their Year 6 primary school all the way through from reception so they had had the opportunity to develop relationships and progress within a stable school setting. Glyn's primary headteacher observed that he was one of the first Traveller students to attend the school all through.

Students mainly moved school due to family movement but other students had changed school for more negative reasons including racial bullying, behaviour problems, and exclusion. Of the seven students who arrived at their primary school in Year 6, one started at Christmas and two in the last term of Year 6 (including one excluded student who attended part time for the last few weeks of term and was taught in isolation by the TES). Thus students within the sample had a range of experiences, with a number having relatively stable primary school experiences and a number who quite clearly had not.

Table 2.1 Length of time students attended their Year 6 primary school

N = 44	Number of students	Number who had not attended school prior to entry
Since reception	17	N/A
Since Y2	6	3
Since Y3	3	1
Since Y4	3	0
Since Y5	8	0
Since Y6	7	0

It is important to examine the number of primary schools attended by students in the study in order to highlight the levels of transience in their primary school experiences. Table 2.2 shows the number of primary schools attended by students in the study.

Table 2.2 Number of primary schools attended by students in the study

Students attending:	Number of students
1 primary school	21
2 primary schools	7
Number unknown but more than 2	6
3 primary schools	4
Number unknown but more than 3	1
4 primary schools	2
5 primary schools	3

Primary schools' experience and expectations of student transfer and retention

The transfer of Traveller students to secondary school was a relatively new experience for the primary schools involved, with just over half (17) having had some experience of student transfer. This was not always a totally successful experience though one head-teacher observed that it had improved over the years and there was an emerging pattern of successful transfer. Ten of the 17 schools highlighted that older siblings of students in the sample had transferred successfully. For some schools transfer was a recent development (Danny and Gemma's older brothers were the first Traveller students to transfer). Other siblings had transferred less successfully, like Billy's two older brothers who had transferred to secondary school but were subsequently excluded. The students' parents had generally not attended secondary school so they were the first generation to transfer. Some primary schools had a relatively small proportion of Traveller students transferring. For example, only a couple of students from Hannah's school had transferred in the past two years despite the fact that this primary school had the highest percentage of Traveller students in the sample (typically ranging between 20-30 per cent over a school year). Transfer was a big issue at this school as in Hannah's year no parents had put in any transfer forms. However, overall there were only two schools with no history of transfer. Just under half of the primary schools were either unable to comment on the expectation of transfer and retention because they had little or no history of Traveller students or no response was given.

Over half (12 of the 20) of the students who were still in school in Year 9 had attended primary schools with experience of Traveller students transferring to secondary school. However, two students in the study who had attended the two primary schools with no history of transfer were also still in secondary school in Year 9. Ten of the 17 primary schools with experience of Traveller students transferring still had Traveller students attending secondary school in Year 9.

Retention of Traveller students at secondary school was more problematic than transfer. Where primary schools were able to comment on the retention of Traveller students, a significant number (9) noted that Traveller students were not being retained in secondary school. Some highlighted limited retention until Year 8 or 9, but this represented a positive development as previously no Traveller students at all had transferred. In five instances they said that retention of Traveller students in secondary school had been successful and in four of these cases it was an older sibling of a sample student who had been retained in secondary school. All those primary schools where interviewees highlighted successful retention at secondary school still had sample students attending in Year 9, so trends were being maintained.

Students who attended primary schools with a relatively high proportion of Traveller children were not more likely to be retained in secondary school: only four of the 14 students attending primary schools with a high proportion of Travellers (more than 10 per cent) were still in school in Year 9.

Primary school interviewees were also asked about their expectation of whether the sample students would transfer to secondary school and be retained. Their responses were fairly accurate: of the 32 students teachers said would successfully transfer to secondary school only two did not. Primary school teachers felt that 13 students from the sample would not be retained in secondary school and this prediction was largely borne out. Only one of these 13 students, Dean, was in school in Year 9, and he had not been retained at his original secondary school but had transferred to a special school. Seven of those students whose primary schools were unsure about their retention were still attending in Year 9, with varying degrees of success.

Preparation and support for parents regarding transfer to secondary school

Parental anxiety

Many parents had an extremely limited experience of primary education and the majority had not attended secondary school; those who had, often had negative experiences of secondary education. Thus, a number of parents were extremely anxious about going into school, even within the relatively 'friendly' context of primary schools. The prospect of their children transferring to secondary school and, in some cases, to a totally unfamiliar context, was especially daunting for Traveller parents. In addition, parents expressed specific cultural anxieties regarding Traveller children's transfer to secondary school. These anxieties have been well documented (Kiddle, 1999) and parents in this study reiterated many of these concerns. Ronnie's mother vocalised a number of these anxieties when she said:

> I don't want him to go to the high school because children are smoking there. They should keep him back I don't want him to be made a fool of because he can't read. He'll pick up bad habits there. Because they know he's a Gypsy they'll make fun of him. They'll put stuff on the board and laugh.

Parental concerns focused on:

- racist name-calling and bullying (14)

- drugs, including smoking and drinking (10)

- mixing with the opposite sex (5)

- sex education (4)

- negative experiences or perspectives of secondary teachers (4)

- concerns about teasing from other Travellers (3)

- lack of academic support in secondary school (2)

- too much perceived freedom or lack of supervision, especially at lunchtime (2)

- concerns that strict attendance monitoring may curtail lifestyle (2).

Parents' responses show that racist name-calling and bullying was a major concern, something that parents felt schools did not take seriously enough (see Chapter 6). However school staff were more likely to suggest that it was Traveller students who were responsible for initiating the name-calling and bullying and that other students were only calling them names in retaliation. This view was prevalent in both primary and secondary phases. Parents felt that their children were responding to other students' racial taunts but that it was the Traveller children who got into trouble. They expressed anxiety that at secondary school this behaviour would be exacerbated.

Parental concerns also reflected a mistrust or rejection of the majority culture (see also Chapter 5) including the perceived detrimental impact of a *gauje* education: sex education, adolescent relationships and drugs, were all seen as problematic by some parents. Non-transfer to secondary school was also seen as a form of cultural protection as highlighted by Hannah's mother: 'If I send her to secondary school she'll be segregated by her own people. She'll be different'. Other factors focused on lack of support for their children's learning needs and siblings' poor experiences at secondary school. Even those parents, like Marie's mother, who were supportive of secondary education, expressed anxiety about their children's safety within school: 'I worry about the kids all day long when they are in school'. In addition, Ben and Chelsea's parents had concerns about prosecution if they did not send their children to secondary school: 'If I thought I could get away with not sending them I wouldn't'.

Parental support

Preparation and support for transfer to secondary school could be crucial in allaying and addressing some of the anxieties and fears expressed by Traveller parents. Parental support raised by interviewees fell into the following categories:

- new parents' evenings/visits

- written information to parents

- TES support

- primary school support

- TES, primary school and/or secondary school liaison/support

- friends and relatives

- siblings on roll.

New parents' evenings and visits provided parents with information about uniform, timetables and school expectations. Thirteen parents indicated that they had been to a parents' evening or visit. In two schools, the parents' evening was actually held at the primary school, thus providing a less intimidating atmosphere for parents in a familiar place. Many of the parents in the sample had not attended secondary school themselves so visiting the schools was seen as significant support for secondary education. The majority of children (11/13) whose parents attended new parents' evenings or visited the school were still in school in Year 9.

A number of parents (9) said that they had not attended new parents' evenings, mainly because they did not want to go (5), but also because they were away travelling at the time (2), they were unaware there was a parents' evening (1), or because they knew what to expect as an older child already attended the school (1). Eleven parents also said that the new secondary schools had sent out written information to them about the school, which would have been problematic for those parents with literacy difficulties.

In some authorities and with particular families, the TES played a significant role in preparation and support for parents regarding transfer. In two LEAs, for example, TES workers said that they were responsible for overseeing the whole process from ensuring that transfer forms were completed and returned on time through to checking that parents had confirmed their acceptance of a place within the necessary timeframe. This was seen as a key area where Traveller students had in the past 'fallen through the net': 'four or five years ago Traveller pupils were not getting their first choice or weren't getting a place at all' (TES teacher). Thus the TES viewed this as a crucial time for targeted support to help ensure transfer:

> We identify all the Year 6 pupils in October and give them information about school transfer over and above what other children normally get. We follow up each application form and ensure they have been returned on time – so that parents actually make their preference known. It means that Traveller children are now going to some of the more popular schools instead of them being allocated a school where there are surplus places. Once allocated they have ten days to confirm in writing their wish to take it up or else they may lose it so again we follow all that up. (TES teacher)

The TES were also addressing additional problems, which in the past, had led to non-transfer:

1. In one LEA Catholic schools had different policies and deadlines for the completion of transfer forms, which could disadvantage some students.

2. If parents did not secure their first choice of secondary school the TES would support the parents through the appeals procedure.

Other TES staff targeted those parents and students who were identified as 'vulnerable' to non-transfer. They were also involved in general awareness raising with both parents and students, regarding the expectation that Traveller students would transfer to secondary school. The TES was seen as a vital source of information about the secondary school, particularly for parents who had not had children transfer to secondary school before. Parents were happy to approach the TES about questions and concerns and also for advice as to which secondary school to choose. Linked to this was work focusing on addressing parental anxieties about transfer such as the learning support available and concerns about children leaving school during the day. The TES offered practical advice and assistance to parents about getting uniform and help with forms for uniform grants if needed. TES staff also accompanied parents and children on school visits if they had missed group visits, or were not confident about going to parents' evenings, or if students were transferring to a different secondary school from other primary students. For those students who moved to a different secondary school after transition, the TES role in organising enrolment and pre-entry visits was seen as crucial both by parents and the schools. TES staff also provided secondary schools with relevant information about families such as parents' literacy difficulties. In a number of instances the TES provided support across the school phases to reassure parents that children would have a familiar adult contact in secondary school.

Primary school preparation and support for parents regarding transfer tended to focus on similar areas to TES support by ensuring that transfer forms were completed and offering assistance with completion, addressing parental anxiety about transfer, helping with uniform and arranging visits to the secondary school. Support for parents also focused on liaison between the primary schools, secondary schools and TES. For example, joint SENCO review meetings were held to discuss students' needs and support at secondary school, and arrangements were made for parents and students to meet with the SENCO prior to transfer. Also, there were examples of liaison between the primary school and secondary school where the primary informed the secondary school of specific parental anxieties and suggested possible solutions.

Parents also said that they received information they needed about secondary schools from friends and relatives who had children at the secondary school and, in some instances, their recommendations had led to students transferring to these schools. Another important source of information for parents about the secondary schools were older siblings or other relatives who had attended or were currently attending the school.

Parental preference: reality or rhetoric?

Parental preference was largely rhetoric: parents theoretically had a choice of schools but in reality because of transport difficulties or other schools being over-subscribed, their choice was relatively limited. In rural areas students could in theory attend a number of secondary schools but in reality most attended the nearest secondary school because parents would have to transport them to the other schools. This constraint on parental choice was an issue both in rural and city locations: 'The option of schools rarely crops up in these rural areas – pupils just go to the nearest one' (TES teacher). 'Ours go to [failing secondary school on Special Measures[1]] whether they want to or not, they have to appeal if they don't want to' (teacher, inner city primary school).

In a number of authorities the TES had taken responsibility for ensuring that transfer forms were completed so that Traveller parents could at least make their secondary school preferences known, whereas previously, Traveller students had either not been allocated secondary school places or when they were allocated a place, it was at a school with surplus places.

Which schools did parents select?

Most parents chose secondary schools which regularly admitted students from the primary schools attended by their children. Nearly three-quarters (31) of the students in the sample transferred to their primary school's main link secondary schools. Although again the concept of parental 'preference' must be questioned, as Leanne's mother commented: 'Well I wouldn't say we chose it as such. They just said it would be [name of secondary school]'.

The key factors identified by parents when selecting a secondary school were:

• siblings or other relatives having attended (23)

• other Traveller students/friends transferring with them (15)

• close to home (10)

• single sex school (1).

More than half (23) the students in the sample were either transferring to schools their siblings were currently attending or had attended in the past (19), or to schools their cousins attended (4). This was generally viewed as a positive factor (particularly if their siblings' experience had been relatively successful). However when the experience had been less successful there was concern that students would be judged according to the behaviour of their brother or sister. In at least four cases students were transferring to schools from which siblings had been excluded or had exhibited behavioural problems. Eight students were transferring to schools where their siblings had a successful experience and had either completed school or were still there, but eleven were transferring to schools where their siblings' experiences had been more mixed and they had left prior to completing Year 11.

Parents also chose secondary schools because they were close to home and easily accessible, although sometimes that was the *only* reason parents had chosen the secondary school: 'If there were another school I wouldn't put him in it [transfer school] but the other schools are too far away' (Christopher's mother). Others saw it as a protective mechanism, wanting their children close by in case they encountered any difficulties: 'I don't mind which one he goes to as long as it's close. In case there's any bullying, I want to be able to get up there' (Kieran's mother). In addition, parents chose schools other Travellers were transferring to, or already attended because cultural support and protection was seen as important. As Clint's mother observed she chose it 'because it's had Gypsies for years'.

A small number of parents (4) stated that their children had chosen the secondary school they were to attend. These were parents who had not attended secondary school themselves so perhaps they felt more confident leaving the decision to their children. Three of the four students were no longer in school in Year 9. This may suggest a link between retention problems and a lack of parental investment in the secondary school. Parents also asked TES advice about possible secondary schools and in some instances the TES were proactive in securing places for Traveller students. In a number of instances (7) Traveller students in the sample were the only students transferring to that particular secondary school, which may have been an isolating factor for some of them.

A total of 42 parents completed transfer forms for secondary school. The remaining two parents opted for Education Otherwise and an alternative education initiative. In terms of school performance analysis of the DfES schools standards performance data (DfES 2002) showed that more than half (22/42) of the students in the sample were due to transfer to secondary schools which performed below the LEA and national average (including four schools which were well below average). Two-fifths (18/42) of students were transferring to secondary schools where performance exceeded the local and national average, and the remaining two students transferred to schools that performed in line with the LEA and national average.

Those parents not selecting the most obvious transfer route and reasons why

Nearly a quarter (12) of the sample's parents did not select the most obvious transfer route to secondary school for their children. The reasons given focused on wanting to send their child:

- to a school with a better reputation than the main transfer school (3)

- to a school nearer to home than the secondary school most primary students were transferring to (3)

- to a secondary school with other Traveller students and where Travellers had successfully transferred in the past (3)

- to a single sex school (1).

For Bernie there was some confusion over the selection of a secondary school. Bernie's mum told the researcher and the TES that she had selected the usual transfer school but the primary school headteacher was adamant that this was not the case. This student did not transfer to secondary school.

Preparation and support for Traveller students

Expectations

Generally students were positive about their transfer to secondary school but like most children they expressed some reservations. Nevertheless, over three-fifths (27) of the students in Year 6 were generally positive about their transfer. Seven students expressed negative expectations about secondary school. The most common concern was relationships with peers, including bullying (6). Of the seven, only Becky was still attending school in Year 9, albeit with behavioural problems, and she had been excluded on a number of occasions.

Did students' expectations reflect those of their parents, or vice versa? In nearly half (21) of the cases they did (17 positive and 4 negative expectations). Of the 17 parents and children who expressed positive expectations about secondary school all but five were in school in Year 9. Three of the four students where both parents and children expressed negative expectations about secondary school were not in school in Year 9.

Overall, negative expectations about secondary school in Year 6 were a relatively good indicator of retention, but what about where expectations diverged? A quarter (11) of the sample's parents expressed more negative expectations of secondary school than their children, whilst four students expressed more negative expectations than their parents. In Year 9 less than half of these students were still in school.

Siblings on roll

Parental and student expectations about secondary school were shaped by older siblings' experience. Other children were happy there, so there was a belief that this child would also be happy: 'I was quite happy with [name of school] because it was fine for the other two' (Shelley's mother).

Conversely, where siblings had a negative experience of the school, parents felt that these students might also have difficulties:

> I'm surprised they let him in at [name of school] because the others left early. I thought they may think 'oh no not another [name of family]'. [Brother] had trouble at [name of school] and I don't want Matthew tarred with the same brush. (Matthew's mother)

Over two-fifths (19) of the students were transferring to schools that siblings had attended, or were currently attending. Eleven of these students had siblings on roll when they transferred to secondary school. All of these students, apart from one who became a school refuser and whose sister was on roll but not attending when she transferred, were still in school in Year 9. Thus, having a sibling on roll at the point of transfer may be an indicator of likely retention (this is explored in Chapter 8).

TES support

TES transfer support for students focused on:

- TES staff working in feeder primary schools and secondary schools to provide continuity of support (16)

- focused transfer work with Year 6s (10)

- initial support (pastoral and/or learning) after transfer into secondary school (10)

- taking students on secondary school visits (5)

- liaison with secondary school regarding students' needs (2)

- arranging school transport (1)

- arranging places on summer schools (1)

- establishing alternative provision linked to the secondary school to try and aid transfer (1).

As can be seen from above the three most common strategies used by the TES in supporting student transfer were:

- Staff working across phases –some TES staff worked in both feeder primary schools and secondary schools to provide continuity of support and hopefully aid transfer: 'I talk a lot about high school, they know I work there and they appreciate that link' (Ronnie's TES teacher). Shelley's TES teacher commenting on the strategy of working across the primary and secondary school added: 'It is difficult to assess objectively whether that is an effective strategy but it certainly helps me to pick up when children aren't going to transfer or might need some support to transfer'.

- Focused transfer work with Year 6 – in one TES there was a nominated transition worker within the team who worked specifically with Year 6 students, especially those who might experience difficulties with transfer. Dean and Christopher's primary headteacher acknowledged the importance of this work, not just for Traveller students, but for all students: 'Transition is a big issue, that's why the work [TES] has done would have been beneficial to a lot more of our children'. Another example of focused transfer work with Year 6s included a TES teacher working with students in school once a week throughout Year 6, which increased to three times a week in the summer term of Year 6 and then the teacher supported them in secondary school for the first half term of Year 7.

- Post-transfer support – this was often used as a monitoring mechanism for TES staff and was generally offered during the first term to 'iron out any problems early on' (Bridget's TES teacher): 'In the first term after transfer I timetable myself in a lesson each week – just as general support not identified to the pupils as TES support for named pupils – that is an excuse for me to be in the school and oversee how things are.' (Eileen's TES teacher).

In a small number (5) of cases TES staff had taken students on secondary school visits either because students were not transferring to the main link secondary school or had missed the main school visit, or parents were too anxious to attend. This was particularly important when parents had little or no experience of secondary school and felt intimidated by all school environments: 'I didn't fancy going to look round – secondary schools are even more scary [than primary schools]' (Eileen's mother). In one instance the TES teacher had taken the student to visit a number of potential secondary schools and described herself as 'proactive' in securing a place at the secondary school (which her brother also attended) although the TES teacher observed that the student 'had a high input into the choice' (Eileen's TES teacher). Interestingly, Eileen did not settle at this secondary school and transferred to the main link secondary school after three weeks.

TES staff also supported students by alerting secondary school staff to students' individual learning needs. Although information would normally be provided by the primary school, TES staff often had additional insights and in one case wanted to continue working with a statemented student in secondary school because of her awareness of his specific needs. In other instances such as Christopher's they alerted secondary school staff to this student's need for additional support even though he was not statemented.

Students' involvement in induction activities

Over three-fifths (27) of the sample had attended some form of induction activity, either a visit to the secondary school with their primary classmates or at new parents' evenings. Over half of the sample (25 students) had attended secondary school visits, usually lasting for a day or two, but in one instance it was a 'trial week': 'we went for a full day to look around, get the uniform and do a few lessons' (Stacey). Four students who were not transferring to one of their primary's recognised link secondary schools had also attended day visits to their prospective secondary schools. Twelve students had attended new parents' evenings, either with their parents, with TES staff, or with friends' or relatives' parents who also had children transferring to the school. Students were generally positive about their visits to the school. As Shelley observed: 'it was really good there were all these demonstrations in the different classrooms ... we met some of the teachers and could speak to the children'. However, Louis' pre-transfer visit was described by the primary headteacher as a 'disaster' because there had been behavioural problems. There were concerns that he would be identified with his cousin (who did have behaviour difficulties) and the school had asked that the secondary school place them in separate classes. This could be seen as an example of a student's individual behaviour being linked by the school to their cultural identity. Four students had also attended summer schools at their new secondary schools which helped them familiarise themselves with their new schools and fellow students before term began.

Seven students did not attend any form of induction activity and none of these students were retained. Three were away when the induction took place, two did not attend, one student was not transferring, and one was going to a different secondary school to his primary classmates. In this case his primary headteacher observed that this had set him apart from his classmates as all the other students had attended a day's induction activity at their secondary school. This student was one of those who did not transfer at all. Of the remaining 11 students, three said they were going on a visit but it is not known whether they did attend and it is unknown whether the remaining eight were involved in any form of induction activity.

Relationships between primary and secondary schools

In terms of preparation and support for both students and parents the quality of the relationship between primary and secondary schools can be seen as a key factor in assisting successful transfer. This relationship may be particularly important for Traveller students whose families have had little experience of transfer to secondary school. Positive relationships between primary and secondary schools can also be seen as facilitating information exchange such as students' learning needs and family contexts, which is also likely to aid transfer and retention. The quality of communication and dialogue is also important. Negative reports from a primary school are likely to influence the secondary school's perception of a student so it is important that the information is accurate. There had been instances in the primary phase where negative reports from previous schools attended by students had possibly impacted on their new schools' views of these students.

In two cases the relationship between primary and secondary schools was described as 'very good'. The headteacher of Matthew's primary school said that the secondary school: 'was given as much information as they are willing to take' and there was a 'long history of liaising with them'. The nature of the relationship and liaison between primary and secondary schools about transfer focused on:

- visits and meetings
- information exchange
- curriculum work including summer schools.

Visits and meetings

Visits and meetings took place at both the primary and secondary schools. In over half (19) of the primary schools secondary school staff visited the primary schools to talk to Year 6 students, sometimes including parents and staff. A range of secondary school staff regularly visited the primary schools to talk to Year 6 students.

Heads of year were most likely to visit but senior managers, learning support staff, SENCOs, department representatives, senior learning support assistants and junior liaison staff were also involved. In Shane's primary school the secondary school head conducted a 'question and answer session' with Year 6 students prior to transfer, and two secondary schools had nominated liaison workers to focus on transfer and visit the primary schools frequently during Year 6. Six of the primary schools also indicated that secondary school SENCOs would visit and attend relevant review meetings and meet parents during Year 6. Secondary school students also visited primary schools to talk to Year 6 students (and parents) about their experiences of secondary school. At least one of the primary schools shared its campus with the secondary school, which improved liaison.

Information exchange

Information on individual students was also exchanged between primary and secondary school staff, either at face to face meetings or via information sheets and 'thumb nail' sketches. The information exchanged focused on gathering data on: attainment (including SATs), support needs, social groupings, behaviour, attitude and attendance. In a number of instances primary school staff were asked for suggestions for social groupings at secondary school so that students could be placed together for peer support.

Curriculum work

Interviewees also highlighted the beginnings of liaison between primary and secondary schools in terms of curricular work. Two secondary schools were involved in bridging work projects in link primary schools, whilst in another primary the head of Year 7 taught the Year 6 class in order to assist in the development of relationships. This relationship was not always seen as a welcome link – one secondary school which was trying to build curricular links with a primary school had experienced some opposition from primary school staff to their involvement in primary classroom activities. The other main curricular link between schools was the literacy and numeracy schools held by secondary schools over the summer for Year 6 leavers.

There were, however, some instances where the relationship between the primary and secondary school was limited or non-existent. This was usually where students were not transferring to the main link secondary school so there was no contact or relationship between the two schools. This was the case for five students in the sample, which perhaps placed them at a disadvantage to their peers and increased the risk of non-transfer. For example, Eileen's Year 6 class teacher was not aware that she was transferring to a different school from the other students in her class. However, there were two instances where students were transferring to link secondary schools but no one from the secondary school had been to visit the primary school. Dean and Christopher's primary headteacher said that he would like to make more positive links with the secondary school and that he had never been able to say to the Year 6 students: 'Isn't it wonderful you're going there? ... We cope with the kids as a small intimate primary school they get down there and the ball game changes'.

Failure to transfer

A total of six students: Louisa, Shannon, Bernie, Samantha, Seamus and Hannah failed to transfer to secondary school, although two of the students did access alternative educational provision. Samantha went on to Education Otherwise and was taught by a home tutor until the end of Year 7, whilst Hannah attended a part time alternative educational provision facilitated by the LEA until the end of Year 8. Three case studies are presented of students who did not transfer (Seamus, Louisa and Hannah) in order to provide some insights into the individual reasons for non-transfer.

Were there any common factors amongst these six students that may have led to them not transferring to secondary school?

Common factors in non-transfer
Cultural factors

Four of the six students were girls and cultural expectations did appear to have some influence on them not transferring to secondary school. Three of the four parents of the girls who did not transfer expressed cultural reservations about their daughters attending secondary school and certainly in Hannah's case this was the main reason why she did not transfer:

Case study 1 Hannah

Hannah was the youngest of three children living on a local authority site. Her mum (a non-Traveller) had attended secondary school but her dad had not. Hannah attended her primary school from reception; the school had a large proportion of Traveller students making up between 20-30 per cent of the school roll. She was fully integrated into school life and participated in extra-curricula activities: she was captain of the netball team, as well as taking lead parts in plays. Her mum was also actively involved with the school and Hannah was open regarding her cultural identity. Her parents were extremely supportive of primary education but not secondary school because of the negative aspects of a *gauje* education. Her two older brothers had attended secondary school for a limited period but their experiences had not been very positive.

She achieved Level 4s[2] in her Key Stage 2 SATs and was particularly good at sport and drama. She did not receive any support from the TES in primary school, except on a pastoral basis. Her attendance in Year 6 was 90 per cent.

No transfer forms were completed by any of the Year 6 Traveller parents at Hannah's primary school. Her parents were happy for her to attend primary school but were adamant that she would not attend secondary school. She attended part time alternative educational provision facilitated by the LEA until the Easter of Year 8 (the provision closed in the summer of Year 8).

Possible factors

- Cultural factors. Parents' concerns about the negative influences of a secondary education meant that Hannah did not transfer.

- Different views were held regarding the purpose of the alternative educational provision: Hannah's parents saw it as an alternative to secondary school, whereas the LEA/TES saw it more as a 'stepping stone' into secondary school. Thus, the alternative provision was unsuccessful because of the different expectations held regarding eventual transfer to secondary school.

Case study 2 Louisa

Louisa was the eldest child in her family which had no history of transfer to secondary school. She moved primary schools at the start of Key Stage 2 because of racial bullying. She did not have many friends and was quite isolated within school. None of the students at her second primary school knew she was a Traveller. Teachers were aware, but mum did not want her identified. Louisa was concerned that her 'cover would be blown' by the TES, and there was a lot of stress about being identified as a Traveller. Louisa felt picked on by some staff because she was a Traveller. Louisa's mum had also been bullied at school and although she was much happier with the second primary school, she felt that if Louisa was identified as a Traveller she would be bullied again.

Louisa made progress at her second primary school; although her attainment was still relatively low she was operating at Level 2 to 3 across all subjects. She was on the SEN register[3] so she also received in-school support. Her attendance was poor at both primary schools (63 per cent in Year 6) and her class teacher said that it was this that set her apart from her classmates.

She received support from the TES throughout primary school apart from a short period after she had moved schools. Her mum was reluctant for Louisa to have TES support because of the risk she would be identified as a Traveller. However because she was struggling academically she agreed for them to go back in. During Year 6 a TES support assistant provided three hours a week support.

The TES felt that in Year 5 there would have been 'no hope' of Louisa transferring due to her previous negative experiences, but that in Year 6 her mother's attitude apparently changed. Louisa was due to transfer, her primary school was confident she would, and the appropriate transfer forms were completed. She was due to transfer to the main link secondary school and her mum said she was looking forward to going although it did not have a very good reputation. However the TES teacher said that a place had been secured at a different school (the one attended by other Traveller children from the site where Louisa lived). She did not transfer to either and there was no communication between home and school. In a follow-up telephone call, Louisa's Mum said that her daughter was staying with relatives.

Possible factors

- Experiences of racial bullying
- Confusion concerning which school she was transferring to, not transferring to a school used by other Traveller students.
- Louisa's mum said she had no input in the choice of secondary school and that Louisa had chosen it

Case study 3 Seamus

Seamus was one of seven children living on a local authority site. There was no history of transfer to secondary school as his four older siblings did not transfer and his parents had no experience of attending school. Seamus had a long period out of school due to racial bullying and he did not start properly until he was eight. His family were extremely protective of him. He was kept back a year because he had missed so much primary education. His brother was in the year below him so he was kept back another year so they could transfer together which meant that he was two years older than his peer group.

Seamus and his two siblings were the only Traveller students in their primary school and they were open about their cultural identity. There had been huge resistance from the school and other parents to their admittance and the family had to go to appeal to get the children in. Once attending, the children were very happy at the school and his parents were delighted with it. Seamus had a statement of special educational neediv with full-time, one to one support from a learning support assistant (LSA) in Year 6. At Key Stage 2 he was operating at a Level 2 throughout. His attendance in Year 6 was '70 per cent plus' which was described by the TES as 'excellent compared with other Travellers'.

His family had close links with the primary school TES but had no links with the secondary school TES (in a different LEA). The TES provided in-class support in primary prior to SNA support and still provided in-class support for his brother. He was transferring to a secondary school in another TES catchment area. At the time of transfer the TES covering the secondary school was having staffing problems: staff had left and new staff had not been appointed. There was no support for students, and all the Traveller students in the LEA stopped attending secondary school. There was therefore no immediate follow up in relation to Seamus not transferring and the secondary school was told that he was in Ireland, so they took him off roll.

His parents were concerned that Seamus would experience racist bullying (again) at secondary school, and that he was too old for school. He was due to transfer to the link secondary school with his brother, cousin and all the students in his Year 6 class. He attended the induction day but did not attend the summer school which his brother went to. His brother and cousin transferred (and retained until Easter Year 7) but he did not.

Possible factors

- Age (he was two years older than his classmates)
- No links with the secondary TES to address possible fears
- Limited follow up from the school regarding his non-transfer
- Family had no relationship with secondary school so no trust established

If I send her to secondary she'll be segregated by her own people she'll be different ... It's not right for Hannah because of her age and the amount of children, she's mixing in with more *gaujes* and less Travellers ... It's not just the sex education it's everything.

Similarly Louisa's mother said: 'We don't like them mixing with boys as they get older. It's a big worry'. However, there was also a culture of non-transfer of Traveller students within Hannah's primary school. This was the primary school with the largest proportion of Traveller students in the sample, but no Year 6 Traveller parents had completed any transfer forms. Samantha's parents also expressed reservations about her transfer to secondary school: 'We are Travelling people and we don't agree with a lot of secondary education, particularly to do with sexual matters' (Sam's father). Both Hannah and Louisa's mothers expected them to be helping them at home when they were 14 or 15 and their daughters concurred with this view. Cultural expectations were also likely to have affected Seamus' non-transfer, especially because of his age; there was a belief that he should be out working with his brothers (see also Chapters 5 and 8).

Racial bullying

Previous experience of racial bullying may have influenced two of the student's non-transfer. Both Seamus and Louisa had experienced quite severe racial bullying in previous primary schools, which had resulted in Seamus not attending school from the age of 5 and a half to eight, and Louisa had changed primary schools at the beginning of Key Stage 2 to get away from the bullying at her previous school. Both students were obviously scarred by their previous experiences and although they had positive experiences in the primary schools they transferred to, they must have been concerned that it might happen again at secondary school. In Louisa's case, the bullies she had escaped from at her previous primary school were going to be attending her secondary school, so there was the potential for them to bully her again but also they could identify her as a Traveller student – something which she had kept hidden as a consequence of the racial bullying. Seamus' mother was also concerned that he would be bullied again when he transferred to secondary school:

'the only thing I'm worried about is the name calling, after his previous experience he won't go'. In addition, Bernie's mother also expressed concern about racial bullying at secondary and said that she would only consider a Catholic secondary school because 'they are stricter on the kids' but the primary school headteacher said that she had chosen a non-Catholic secondary school.

Confusion concerning which secondary school they were transferring to

There was some confusion over which secondary school both Louisa and Bernie were transferring to. In Bernie's case the TES teacher and his mother said he was going to the main link Catholic secondary school with all the other students in his class but the primary school headteacher said that Bernie's mother had applied for him to go to a different school, that he would be the only student from his school going there and that he had been set apart because of this. Similarly, staff at Louisa's primary school were under the impression that she was transferring to the main link secondary school but the TES had been informed by her mother that she would be transferring to another secondary school, which other students from the site attended.

Late starters

Three of the six students were late starters, both Samantha and Seamus had not started school until Year 3, and Shannon had started in Year 2 'after a lot of persuasion ... mum very nervous'.

Attainment and attendance

Students' attainment and attendance was relatively mixed, which makes it difficult to associate either of these factors with their non-transfer. Four of the six did have low levels of attainment: Seamus was statemented, Samantha and Louisa were functioning at Level 2/3 and were on the SEN register, and Shannon was operating below Level 2 and was on Stage 3[5] of the Code of Practice. However, there were other students in the sample who were achieving at similar levels who did transfer successfully. Hannah and Bernie were operating at higher levels. Hannah achieved Level 4 across all subjects and Bernie was the first Traveller student in his school to achieve a Level 4 (in science). Their attendance also ranged from 90 per cent in Year 6 for Hannah, to 70 per cent plus for Seamus, to 63 per cent for Louisa. Shannon's attendance was described as 'good for Travellers' and Bernie's was a 'bit erratic but better than some other Traveller pupils'. Thus, it is difficult to suggest that these students' rates of attendance at primary school were linked to their non-transfer.

Other factors

A number of other factors were explored which may have impacted on non-transfer including the number of primary schools attended by the students, the length of time they were at their Year 6 primary schools and their siblings' experience. There did not appear to be any common factors.

Points for reflection

- What measures might be taken to ensure the effective monitoring of Traveller students' transfer from primary to secondary school, particularly when the schools are located in different LEAs or students are not following the normal transfer routes? There is a need for clearer lines of communication and information exchange between the TESs and schools involved so that students do not slip through the net.

- Could more be done to ensure that Traveller parents are able to make an informed choice about the secondary schools their children attend and that they complete transfer forms? The practice of TESs checking that transfer forms have been completed would help.

- With the increasing numbers of Traveller parents opting for Education Otherwise what strategies does the LEA have to monitor such arrangements?

- Evidence from the study has shown that alternative provision is not necessarily a stepping stone into secondary school and that the parents' and the TES/schools' expectations need to be the same.

- What measures might be taken to ensure that Traveller parents' concerns about secondary school, particularly in relation to racial bullying and other cultural factors are addressed?

- To what extent does intensive transfer work with Year 5 and 6 students and their families aid transfer and retention of Traveller students? Such input might help raise expectations amongst families, schools and students and also provide opportunities to address issues and concerns.

- How can relationships between Traveller families and secondary schools be established prior to transfer? Transfer might be eased by the development of trusting relationships, along with the maintenance of support networks that have been established in the primary phase.

- Would transfer be improved by the presence of an identified link person in secondary school who is available for parents, students and TES staff to contact if they experience difficulties?

- What measures might be taken to ensure that if a student does not transfer to secondary school there is immediate follow up?

Notes

1   Schools may be placed on Special Measures by Ofsted where standards are judged to be unacceptable

2   Level 4 is the expected standard of attainment for 11 year olds

3   Between 1994 and 2001 the Special Educational Needs Code of Practice required all schools to maintain a register of pupils with SEN.

4   A statement of SEN may be issued after a full and detailed assessment of a pupil's learning difficulties. This was known as Stage 5.The statement details the nature of centrally funded additional support to be provided over and above that which schools are expected to provide for all pupils.

5   Stage 3 of the Code of Practice denoted that external agencies/specialist support was required

3

Oaks and Willows – secondary school responses

This chapter focuses on the responses of the participating secondary schools and examines the extent to which they recognised the challenges facing the Traveller students who transferred and how they responded to their individual and cultural needs. It also explores whether a cultural pathology encourages low expectations regarding attendance, conduct and, ultimately, achievement.

The size, nature and organisational structure of secondary schools can present social and emotional challenges for any student transferring from primary school. Students who enjoyed a secure and harmonious relationship with their primary school teachers may suddenly feel invisible or anonymous. Expectations in terms of self-organisation, homework and uniform requirements tend to be higher than in the primary phase (Nicholls and Gardner 1999). Furthermore, established patterns of friendship may be disturbed and redefined as students move from Key Stage 2 to Key Stage 3. As discussed in the previous chapter, these challenges can be intensified for Traveller students, for whom previous knowledge of the secondary school culture can be very limited. Only twelve of the parents said that they (or their partners) had been to secondary school themselves and for some of these it had been only for a few weeks. Just under half of the children (20) were breaking new ground by being the first in their families (and sometimes in their communities) to transfer. In many cases (as reported in Chapter 2) Traveller parents required a great deal of support and encouragement to enable the transfer to take place. This was attributed largely to the protection of students' physical, psychological and moral well-being. Fears about bullying and racism were uppermost in parents' list of concerns, followed by anxiety about exposure to drugs and sexuality. There can be a delicate balancing act between maintaining high standards and expectations for all students whilst respecting individual needs and differences. As one headteacher explained:

> Our willingness to be flexible is quite important. It is a bit like ... it's not an oak tree, we are not rigid ... we are more like a willow, prepared to bend a little bit. But we're not going to go too far. I think we get the respect of parents because of that and we get the respect of children (secondary headteacher).

The metaphor of oaks and willows is interesting and has been put to use in analysing attitudes and processes in schools (see page 00).

Attendance

The issue of irregular or non-attendance by Traveller students, parti-cularly those of secondary school age, has been consistently flagged up for over thirty years (Plowden, 1967; Reiss, 1975; Swann, 1985; Ofsted, 1996, 1999; DfEE, 1999a). Despite this awareness and the mechanisms introduced recently to raise attendance levels generally, the situation for Traveller students has barely improved and remains an area of 'grave concern' (Ofsted, 2001). The more obvious diffi-culties related to mobility of life style and educational continuity and access have often been the focus of discourse around the issue of attendance – and rightly so. However, such a focus may divert atten-tion away from other factors associated with irregular attendance.

The experience of students in this study certainly corroborates these earlier concerns about attendance. Remember, that although a small minority of the families in the sample had retained a mobile life-style, most were settled on private or local authority sites or in hous-ing. Yet, of the 44 students in the study, over three-quarters (34) were identified as having attendance problems at some point during Key Stage 3. And over two-thirds (24) of the group of poor attendees had left the education system completely by Year 9, showing an association between a pattern of sporadic or declining attendance and a lack of retention in secondary school.

If we begin by looking at the ten students in the study who attended school regularly throughout, we find no obvious trends in relation to gender or attainment. Levels of parental literacy were variable, distance between home and school ranged from less than half a mile to twelve miles and the students were as likely to live in houses as on Traveller sites (including two students who lived on unofficial sites). Having an older brother or sister who had transferred successfully to secondary school was a recurring theme, but the most notable common factor was that the best attendees were almost all described by their teachers as being 'popular' and 'good mixers' with a secure network of non-Traveller friends in school. In other words, strong relationships with other students and a secure sense of self appeared to be predominant features. This concept is explored more fully in Chapters 5 and 8, and may also pertain to the experiences of the students with identified attendance problems.

As far as schools were concerned, Traveller students' attendance was generally felt to be in need of improvement. Not only did poor or irregular attendance adversely affect levels of student attainment, it also suppressed the school's overall attendance statistics, both of which had to be published and were therefore available for scrutiny. Parents, students and Traveller Education Service employees had all noticed a discernible sharpening of school procedures for monitoring and following-up non-attendance: 'Now it's being followed up whereas in the past, Traveller parents knew they wouldn't be followed-up' (TES liaison officer).

Recording non-attendance
The T code
According to the School Attendance Regulations (DFE, 1994) where Traveller students are away travelling for periods of time, in connection with their parents' work or for cultural events such as traditional horse fairs, then such absences may be authorised by schools and recorded as a 'T' in the register. Other absences for genuine reasons such as illness or days of religious observance should be noted in accordance with the Regulations and may also be authorised

by the school. Unjustified or unexplained absences should be deemed unauthorised in the usual way. The interviews revealed some discrepancy in the use of the T code. For example, on examining the register during one interview, Carly's head of year was nonplussed by the fact that her absences were routinely being marked with a T even when she was not travelling or attending cultural events. In this case, the code 'T' was apparently being used to explain any absence by a Traveller student. In another case, a primary headteacher refused permission for Louisa to visit a traditional horse fair because he saw no educational value in it. The visit went ahead regardless and Louisa's mother explained the absence as a bout of illness. Eileen's mother could not understand why she should have to keep explaining her daughter's absences when, according to her understanding, Travellers were legally entitled to have an extra six weeks off, even though the family no longer travelled. Two headteachers complained about the detrimental effect of students' travelling on the school attendance figures. However, the Traveller students concerned rarely left the area and admitted to the researcher that they truanted. Louis' headteacher was not sure about the procedure for taking Traveller students off the roll after a period of unexplained absence and, in a few cases, the T code did not even appear as a recognised category of absence on attendance printouts. These examples suggest the need for greater clarity on the use of the T code and a higher level of awareness of Attendance Regulations.

Obtaining parental notification

Legally, it is up to schools to decide whether or not an absence can be authorised. Verification from parents is usually required in writing and this, in itself, can present a challenge when dealing with parents who may not have competent literacy skills. In some cases, low expectations were communicated by teachers and seemed to perpetuate the problem: 'They don't ask me to bring a note 'cos they know they'll not get it anyway' (Kimberley).

A form tutor in a different school admitted:

> I don't always seek the note from home or the phone call because I know they [Travellers] have mobiles and they might not be switched on.

Thus low expectations may result in a higher incidence of un-authorised absence. Some schools or individual tutors responded more proactively and had developed alternative systems such as pro-viding parents with a template that simply required a signature and a one-word explanation. Others were satisfied with a verbal explana-tion if parents couldn't write. Overall, parents in the study knew that they needed to provide a reason for their child's absence to satisfy the school's procedures, even though it might be difficult. Where schools were seen as being less than sympathetic about cultural commitments, pastoral concerns or alleged bullying, it could be easier for parents to justify absences as being illness-related (like Louisa, above). Some form tutors said that they authorised absences even though the authenticity of the explanation was in doubt. One said that as long as he got some kind of explanation, he wouldn't 'make an issue of it.' Another said 'I do authorise it sometimes ... be-cause I know they go to funerals and there might be prayer meetings and lots of things going on'.

Lateness

Attendance figures can also be adversely affected by students' late-ness and this was another area of concern expressed by some inter-viewees. Some form tutors were fairly relaxed about lateness: 'his parents have to drop siblings off, it's not a problem'. Others were less so, and this inflated the student's absence record. According to official guidance (DfEE, 1999b) schools have some flexibility in terms of how long registers can be kept open. Louis' form tutor, for example, kept the register open until the start of the first lesson, to give Louis a twenty-five minute buffer zone and thus protect him from the automatic detention rule for having two 'lates' in a week. In Chelsea's case, there were circumstances beyond the family's control that impacted on her attendance figures, as her mother ex-plained:

> The school bus is late most of the time but they still mark her down as late. They still put that in the report. '65 Lates' I says 'what you on about? She gets on the bus. But it is the school bus that's late'.

Monitoring attendance

Recent studies (Ofsted 2001; DfES 2003) agree that the systematic follow-up of student absence is a crucial factor in improving attendance patterns. A number of the schools in the study had introduced a system of first day contact with parents. Interestingly, this approach appeared to offer some reassurance to Traveller parents that their children's welfare was being taken seriously. Parents wanted to know that their children were at school and not roaming the streets. The fact that Clint was skipping odd lessons was brought to everyone's attention when his brother arrived unannounced at the school one day to collect a key from him and Clint could not be found anywhere in the building. His parents' trust and confidence in the school as a place of safety was challenged. The school responded by setting up a monitoring programme but Clint left school halfway through Year 8. Not all schools in the study adopted immediate follow-up. Instead, letters would be sent to parents on the third day of absence or a referral would be made to the head of year. In some cases this was justified in terms of limited resources or the impracticality of contacting large numbers of parents. Other schools overcame this problem, however, by operating first day contact for a list of targeted students who were considered to be high-risk attendees.

Heads of year were generally satisfied with the support they received from Education Welfare Officers but there was a view amongst TES staff that schools tended to rely upon their service as the main source of follow-up due to the perception that they had a closer relationship with families. This issue was also highlighted in the 2001 Ofsted report (*Managing Support for the Attainment of Children from Ethnic Minority Groups*). Best practice in that study was characterised by schools which developed trust and good relationships with Traveller parents and did not rely on the TES to always act as a go-between. Typically, TES workers involved the LEA EWO when their efforts had failed and they needed to 'raise the stakes'.

> You have to ensure children have their entitlement. And sometimes, a caution has the desired outcome (TES teacher).

Differences in professionals' expectations about monitoring and follow-up also surfaced. Interestingly, TES staff were more inclined to feel that schools were insufficiently rigorous in their monitoring of Traveller student absences. However, as one deputy headteacher said, it could be difficult to achieve the right balance when expectations were unclear. Sometimes the TES co-ordinator would say to her that the Traveller children needed 'more leeway because of their culture' and at other times demanded to know 'why aren't you getting education welfare onto them?' She told the researcher:

> I never quite know where to go with it and neither does [name of TES teacher assigned to the school]. And sometimes we have a good old moan and say 'What are we supposed to be doing?'

Significantly, three-quarters of the children who left school before the end of Key Stage 3 were reported as having a history of attendance problems. Patterns of poor attendance which are established in the primary phase, therefore, may be difficult to change.

Carrots and sticks

Although the introduction of incentive schemes (such as attendance prizes) can be helpful in raising attendance (Kinder and Wilkin, 1997), this approach is grounded in the assumption that students choose to absent themselves and unless the incentive outweighs the motive for non-attendance, it is unlikely to be effective. The use of group incentives such as inter-form competitions for attendance perhaps needs to be weighed against the potential risk of alienation that Traveller students (or any others) might face if they are seen to have let the form down. One tutor interviewed even admitted to falsifying the register so that the Traveller student in his form group did not jeopardise the opportunity for the class to win a certificate. Some students may have little choice in whether or not they attend. Where family commitments take priority students can find themselves caught between conflicting expectations (see Chapter 5).

Clint, Sarah-Jane and Christopher were all offered reduced timetables of two to three days a week during Year 8 in an attempt by their schools to sustain their engagement in schooling. All three had been exhibiting clear signs of disaffection and sporadic attendance. Teachers justified the arrangement by proposing that any education was better than none. Linda was placed on a reduced timetable of

one and a half days a week after a long period out of education because of her mobile lifestyle. For these four students, however, the
cultural 'pull' apparently outweighed the 'carrot' of part-time attendance and none of them completed Key Stage 3.

Some students and parents interviewed pointed out the perceived un-
fairness of being followed up for non-attendance when other
Traveller children they knew locally were not enrolled in school at
all and appeared to get away with it. Parents felt aggrieved that
despite their best efforts to get their children into school, they were
the ones who were being penalised and not their neighbours:

> It seems unfair 'cos there's about fifteen other children on this
> site who don't go at all and yet they keep going at me!

The students themselves might also be resentful of the local
Traveller children who were not at school. Two sets of parents in the
study were eventually threatened with prosecution but neither case
was heard in court. Both applied for Education Otherwise.

Analysing non-attendance

School interviews and scrutiny of attendance printouts for students
in this study revealed a high incidence of medical absence in some
cases. For example, one student had made ten separate visits to the
medical room in one term, asked to be sent home and missed
twenty-one teaching sessions. Although medical absences were
authorised by the schools, some concerns were expressed about the
prevalence of such absences and in some cases their authenticity.
Heads of year seemed to accept there was little they could do under
those circumstances. 'You can't very well ring up and say 'Sorry, but
can she not be sick!' Official guidance on attendance states that if
the authenticity of illness is in doubt, schools and EWOs could
contact the School Health Service or the student's GP, but no
examples of this type of follow-up were encountered during the
study. One head of year complained that the EWO would not get involved with medical absences at all. The point worth making here is
that although a pattern of medical absence may be entirely genuine,
it may also signal emotional difficulties, perhaps related to bullying
(see Chapter 6) or condoned truancy. The following examples
illustrate how students' psychological well-being can be overlooked:

- Ben's head of year admitted: 'I'm not sure whether to believe it when mum says he is ill ... I'm sure she keeps him off because it's easy'. These reservations were not without foundation although the motive was misinterpreted. Ben's mother admitted to the research team that she kept him off because he was desperately unhappy there but just told the school that he was poorly. Ben did not complete Key Stage 3.

- Becky also told the researcher that she used illness as a strategy for avoiding unhappiness at school. 'I do like coming to school, it's just that it gets me down sometimes and I just take days off. The people get me down, picking on me ... I used to make up excuses to teachers like saying I was sick and I wasn't'. Becky's mother empathised and sometimes condoned absences.

- David had a history of medical absences and had been subjected to bullying. His teachers felt that he was feigning illness in order to get sent home; he even resorted to making himself physically sick. David eventually admitted to using this tactic but his motives were never completely understood. Staff believed that he 'would just rather be at home'.

- Dean's mother said: 'I used to dread mornings. He'd start the night before [saying] 'I don't feel well'. He used to say he'd been sick and they'd send him home. I had to say to them 'Please don't send him home, he's playing up'.

- Joe started missing the same day each week, saying that he felt dizzy and sick. When his mother took him to the doctor's surgery, and the GP started to ask him about school, Joe became upset but denied he was having problems.

There is little doubt that some children in the study were unhappy in secondary school. This predicament also placed their parents under enormous emotional stress. One student presented with school phobia and others engaged in daily emotional battles with their parents in their attempt to avoid school. These parents described how they felt worn down by the experience and ultimately gave in. For example:

> I've tried and I've tried and I've bitter tried, till I've made myself poorly with it.

> It's terrible now. Her father took her in the motor and then he had to turn round and bring her back because she wouldn't get out the motor.

Data from this study suggest that Traveller students can become trapped in a cycle of alienation. Unhappiness in school may be due to unharmonious relationships (the prevalence and nature of bullying and racial harassment is covered in Chapter 6) or inability to access the curriculum (see also Chapter 8). Non-attendance may provide temporary respite but difficulties can be intensified upon return to school as peer contact and curriculum access is disrupted and the cycle perpetuated. Unless the cycle of alienation is noticed and addressed in a prompt and sensitive way, the outlook for retention in school is bleak (see Chapter 7). Unfortunately, teachers and students did not always welcome Traveller students back after a period of absence. Joe spoke about teachers 'getting on' at Traveller students, and demanding to know where they'd been. Becky's TES teacher supported her by taking her back into school after a spate of bullying towards her by other girls. She was incredulous at the reaction of the head of year who was abrasive and made what she thought unnecessary personal comments. Teachers observed the effect that regular absence had on peer relationships: 'the other kids call them 'skivers' and that causes friction'.

Attendance problems could also arise when home-school relationships became strained after a behavioural incident or an imposed sanction. One TES fieldworker described it as 'different streams of logic' resulting in an *impasse*. Schools expected parents to be concerned enough to make an appointment to negotiate re-entry whereas Traveller parents may have felt too intimidated by the prospect (particularly if they had limited experience of secondary schools) or humiliated that their child had been 'rejected' by the school. Where this occurred, it was often the TES who stepped in and tried to mediate.

> They say they send out letters and she [Kenny's mum] doesn't get them, and I don't know whether they do send them – she can't read any way. I have to push and cajole for them to go and visit her, and one of her complaints would be, 'Well they have sent him home and I have heard nothing since!' and she is absolutely right. Until I instigate. 'What is happening with

Kenny then?' They say, 'He stormed off!' I say, 'Yes, well, now what is happening? He has been out a week. Are you contacting Mum? Have you sent a letter? Have you informed the EWO?' and I get blanks. (TES teacher).

As Atkinson *et al* (2000) postulate effective strategies for raising attendance should include preventative measures as well as reactive responses. Proactive intervention requires a reflective approach and a willingness to consider the underlying causes of non-attendance, a point emphasised recently by the DfES (2003). A more reflective response certainly worked in the case of two girls in the sample who had poor school attendance records. Their feelings of low self-worth had also led to a pattern of relationship problems and behavioural concerns. However, by Year 9 both the girls had made a substantial improvement in their attendance and were described as 'happier' after their schools recognised the characteristics of low self-esteem and implemented intervention programmes for them. One school developed a personal skills group in which students learned how to interact more positively with one another and were presented with individual and team challenges to enhance self-esteem. In the other school, a programme of individual tutorials allowed the student to identify problems through a subject review, which led to higher levels of support and the benefit of anger management sessions. Both girls were allocated mentors.

As these examples illustrate, reasons for non-attendance may be complex. Rather than considering the student (and/or the parent) as the object to be addressed and put right, it might be more helpful for schools, LEAs and Traveller Services to adopt an ecosystemic approach, as described by Bronfenbrenner (1979). Greater consideration of the hierarchy of systems ranging from the micro (the individual child) to the macro (cultural and social values in wider society) could promote a better understanding of all the situational and interactional factors that may be responsible for non-attendance.

The cameo on page 00 illustrates the complexity of issues from different perspectives.

Analysing the predicament of non-attendance from different perspectives and sub-systems might encourage joint problem solving and a critical review of policy and practice. Above all, it should

Glyn had been happy and well behaved in primary school but both he and his parents were fearful about transferring to the local secondary school. Racial tension between the white and Asian population ran high in the neighbourhood and a police van was often parked outside at the end of the school day because of inter-racial and gang conflict. The school was in special measures. Staff morale was low and turnover was high. Glyn started school two weeks into the term as the family was travelling. He found it hard to settle and his behaviour and attendance began to deteriorate in Year 7. Although Glyn was able, he was placed in low attainment groups because he required additional support for his behaviour difficulties. Glyn said he hated school. He wore big gold rings to protect himself because of the all the fights. He began to get temporary exclusions. His parents couldn't understand why some days he was being sent home yet on other occasions the school was demanding to know where he was. They felt this was a contradiction. Glyn's attendance got worse and eventually his parents were told that they were to be prosecuted. Glyn's mother claimed that her son was 'frightened for his life' at school. It was affecting his nerves. She herself had witnessed a fight outside the schools gates one morning with students armed with planks of wood and was determined not to send her younger daughter to the same school. Glyn's mother applied for Education Otherwise half way through Year 8 before court proceedings took place. According to the TES, Education Otherwise had become a form of 'official truancy' that had 'fallen into the Travellers' laps'. Glyn's mother saw little value in secondary education anyway as 'no one's going to employ Gypsy boys.'

increase opportunities for meaningful dialogue between all parties. As one TES teacher pointed out: 'We have got to address attendance, and we are addressing attendance ... now we have got to go one step further and *really* look at it!'

Behaviour

Data collected during the latter part of Year 6 and the beginning of Year 7 revealed that behaviour was deemed to be good for the vast majority of students in the study. This includes the six students who failed to make the secondary school transfer and who were all described as 'well behaved' by their primary school teachers. Seamus would 'come so humbly and ask with three pleases for the stapler'. Louisa 'tried so hard to please everyone' and Shannon was a 'perfectly behaved and very kind' member of the class. Despite this general perception, when Year 6 class teachers were asked to predict the challenges the children might encounter in secondary school, they identified the following reservations in addition to attendance:

- Secondary school teachers might challenge the student in an arbitrary, hostile or aggressive manner, provoking the student to respond in a volatile way.

- Secondary school teachers might misinterpret the student's open and direct communication style as a sign of disrespect.

- Students with learning difficulties might be grouped with, and come under the influence of, other students who have additional behavioural difficulties.

- Students with lower ability might employ acting-out behaviours in order to mask their difficulties or to gain peer approval.

- Students might find it difficult to relate to a large number of adults in the school and might not have a trusted adult to whom they could turn in times of difficulty.

- Students might challenge (or be challenged by) others to fight to determine the 'pecking order'.

In relation to the final point, only four Year 6 teachers mentioned the issue of racial bullying overtly, despite the fact that they had known about students' previous experiences of this and were aware that physical retaliation was a common reaction. For some students the first days and weeks in secondary school were blighted by experiences of racial taunting and bullying (see Chapter 6), which resulted in physical retaliation, subsequently described as a 'minor brush' or 'blip' by the teachers. It is also worth noting the negative view that primary school teachers held of teacher-student relationships and teaching styles in the secondary phase.

> You hear of some kids being excluded who were just lovely when they were here. Will he [Charlie] be counselled or challenged aggressively I wonder?

> If she [Samantha] puts one foot out of line, she could be pounced on and I'm not sure how she would take it.

> I know Billy so well that I know how to handle him. I divert him and give him a job to do. But there ... it could be 'stick to the rules or you're out!

Most Year 6 teachers felt that they knew their students very well and often their predictions were subsequently borne out. As the students progressed through Year 7 and into Year 8, their behaviour was increasingly seen as challenging.

Teacher-student relationships

In several cases, the emergent behaviour was contextual rather than generic, suggesting that the relationship with the teacher was a determining factor. Some students had very mixed progress reports in Years 7 and 8, with glowing comments interspersed with extremely negative appraisals of their behaviour. Interviews revealed that where teachers allegedly challenged or rebuked students in a hostile manner, the Traveller students (and their parents) felt this was inappropriate and showed their disapproval accordingly.

> They don't know how to speak to Traveller or Gypsy children. They shout and tell them what to do but they [the children] don't like to be bossed. They don't like to be ordered. If they ask them nicely it's a different thing but if they tell them and boss them they're wasting their time (Glyn's mother).

> If you snap at him he'll say to you 'I'm not a dog' and he'll retaliate back that way and his mouth gets him into a lot of trouble (Kenny's mother).

Some heads of year attributed this type of response to cultural factors rather than assertiveness skills and did not always see the student's point of view:

> He has always got an answer! He'll say 'Well they [the teacher] said this to me and I'm not being spoken to like that.' That is how they [Traveller students] look at it.

> They should expect to be shouted at if they've done something wrong but they take it that their parents are the only ones allowed to discipline them and they will just walk away.

In other cases, heads of year did show more insight into the difficulties and had arranged for students to change forms or teaching groups in order to avert the problem. This showed an acceptance that not all colleagues possessed effective behaviour management and interpersonal skills and the students sometimes had good reason to object to their treatment. Overall, the students generally liked the teachers and there were more positive comments about them than negative ones. Students were clear about which teachers they disliked. These were the ones that shouted at them and showed a lack of respect. Stephen gave this example:

> Some teachers are very kind to me but some are evil and one teacher said 'Get him out before I string him up!' and I replied, 'I have a name!'

A minority of students believed that some teachers held and exhibited racist attitudes about Travellers. These are discussed in Chapter 6.

Having a trusted and understanding adult in the school was especially important for vulnerable students who lacked strong peer support in school. Crystal and Kieran both developed good relationships with their TES teachers who provided continuous support for them from Year 6 until the end of Year 9. Crystal's teacher felt that he had become an anchor point for her and was someone to tell when there'd been an injustice or when she wasn't coping too well. Her form tutor agreed:

> Crystal's self esteem was quite low ... but then Richard [TES teacher] came in, which was fantastic and it really helped boost her confidence. It's nothing really, a fleeting visit but it means so much to Crystal and it supports her so much.

Kieran's teacher felt that she provided a sounding board for helping Kieran to deal with problems or worries. Becky had a mentor and an education social worker to help her with a range of personal difficulties, whilst Marie developed a close relationship with her English teacher.

> This may sound silly but she's given me more confidence. Like when it comes to standing up in front of the class. She said to me 'Look you're as good as any of them and better than some of them, so do it!' She sorts everything out for me!

School rules

The students and their parents were generally accepting of the school rules and understood the need for clear boundaries. Even strict uniform codes were endorsed in principle. Most schools took a strong line on the wearing of earrings for example. Typically, students were permitted to wear studs but not hoops, on the grounds of health and safety. One headteacher was strongly advised by the TES teacher to respect Traveller culture in relation to the wearing of jewellery as there had been legal test cases. Initially, this caused confusion amongst the staff but the rule was reviewed and was justified in terms of health and safety requirements. This was then explained to the parents and there were no further issues. The cultural significance of gold jewellery items was also emphasised by Gemma's mother, who believed that schools should be more understanding in this respect but complied reluctantly with her daughter's primary school's request and by Joe's mother who explained how jewellery is used to mark cultural identity:

> My sister's boy insisted on wearing his gold Travellers' rings to school. Their way is ... it was bought by his dad so he must wear them. These are very important to the boys because it's their identity [in the shape of a horse saddle]. My way is different. I told Joe not to wear his – I said 'what is the best thing? Wearing it to school for the sake of saying I've got this ring or saving it at home for a special occasion?' They're precious and there is a time and a place for everything. I don't think school is the place (Joe's mother).

Another headteacher explained that it was important not to have too many hard and fast rules. Jewellery was permitted as long as it was 'discreet and appropriate' and did not breach health and safety regulations. According to this headteacher, 'we are not going to go around spending all our time picking up kids on jewellery infringements! There are more serious things, like bullying and aggression, to deal with'.

Sanctions

Although most day-to-day rules and expectations were respected by students and their parents, there was much less acceptance of the sanctions that schools employed, as these could be seen as unfair or unrealistic. Imposed isolation from other students was considered unethical: 'that's like prison ... they like to be where they can see out, not to be put in there. Caging them like animals!' After-school detentions were also likely to be challenged. Although several of the students had never been given a detention, those who had were quite likely to have received it for non-completion of homework. In most cases, schools used lunchtime detentions but where after school detentions were given, students sometimes chose to ignore them. Furthermore, parents encouraged this attitude, thus challenging school procedures and presenting staff with the dilemma of how to respond:

> If Ben doesn't do his homework, he will not stay after school, partly because it's difficult for [mum] to get him home, but she is adamant that he is not going to have any sort of punishment. That makes it slightly awkward because he is then not being seen to be treated the same and other students say 'If he can get away with it, why shouldn't I?' (head of year).

Staff in some other schools mentioned similar scenarios and expressed reluctant acceptance of the situation.

> We know the circumstances, they can't do detentions and I'm sure staff take that into consideration before issuing anything out (head of year).

> We don't give them [the Traveller students] after school detentions because of transport problems (form tutor).

Such inconsistent application of rules might be seen (by other staff, students and parents) to be divisive and unjust. Transport difficulties and parental commitments can make after school detentions difficult for any student in a school. The motive for varying the school response may be the avoidance of a confrontation with Traveller parents. This in itself suggests stereotyped expectations and a need for improvement in home-school relationships. Schools which had good relationships with Traveller parents encouraged face to face dialogue with them and were more confident in explaining and justifying their use of sanctions.

Curriculum

Access

Sometimes the deterioration in behaviour was linked to difficulties in accessing the curriculum. Leanne, Kieran and David all had identified learning difficulties but received regular learning support and completed Key Stage 3. David was disapplied from modern foreign language lessons and had booster classes in key skills instead. In Year 9, Kieran was placed in a targeted group which was taught by a small selected group of skilled specialist teachers and received continuous support in every lesson. Part-time college place-ment was part of the Year 10 package and it was anticipated that he would take a combination of GCSEs and Youth Awards. Kieran's head of year emphasised that this was 'not a group for naughty kids. It is composed of those who have specific learning needs and who benefit from working in a secure and non-pressured environment.' Leanne had arrived at secondary school with a statement of her learning difficulties and was included in an intensive literacy pro-gramme. By Year 9, she had moved out of the lower sets and was expected to achieve GCSEs across the curriculum. Additionally, in Year 7, all three students were taught in mixed attainment groups and developed supportive friendships with students across the attainment range. These three students seemed to make a conscious effort to distance themselves from students of a similar level of attainment who had additional behavioural difficulties.

However, other students with special needs may not have been so well supported. These students became disruptive and attended school less frequently. Stephen's specific learning difficulties were not identified until his behaviour had become a serious concern: 'He walks out of lessons, looking around, saying 'Why haven't I got any help?' Dean's coping strategy was to run out of lessons and refuse to attempt the work set and 'if he didn't have the support he just used to wander round the corridors or wander off home.' Christopher's learning difficulties should have warranted a statement according to his TES teacher, but the collection of evidence required for a statutory assessment was thwarted by his increasingly poor atten-dance. There were other examples where students were unable to access their entitlement to support, because the agency concerned was allegedly unwilling to get involved. Charlie's teacher said the learning support service was reluctant to offer help. For Carly, it was the behaviour support service that apparently 'didn't want to know' when asked for help in overcoming her school phobia. The justifica-tion for this lack of involvement was not specified. Perhaps there was an assumption that support for Traveller students was an in-efficient use of resources if their attendance record was poor or that additional support was the responsibility of the TES.

> It's very difficult to get the Educational Psychologist to sanction one-to-one help for Traveller children, who are possibly not

going to be here for very long. They have a history of being non-attenders. The EPS is so strapped for cash that they're not very helpful when it comes to Traveller children (head of year).

I think when children don't attend very well, there is a disinclination on the part of the school to ask external agencies to come in – when they might turn up and the child is not there. I think they might see that the child's poor attendance is a reason for them not attaining. And so you get to a stage where they think, what is the point? And we have to try to counter that as much as we can (TES teacher).

This suggests that systems and mechanisms for providing additional support for students with SEN may be insufficiently flexible to meet the needs of students whose attendance is irregular and may therefore affect Traveller students disproportionately.

Homework

The students found the demands of homework quite difficult to deal with in the first few weeks after transfer. In many cases, the students knew about homework clubs at their school but few took advantage of them. Unless the clubs were held at lunchtimes students were highly unlikely to attend. In one case, homework support was set up especially for a group of Traveller boys who were subjected to peer pressure on the site from other lads who would bang on the side of the caravan as they tried to complete homework. The head of year arranged for the boys to work in school at the end of the day but this arrangement quickly broke down as the students felt they were being punished by staying after school. Two members of staff in this school 'the old hard-line traditionalists' saw this to be preferential treatment and could not empathise with the boys' predicament. A general lack of awareness and understanding of the practical difficulties facing some Traveller students was evident in other cases too. For Shane, whose traditional outdoor lifestyle (on roadside encampments) meant that conditions were not conducive to home study, the problem became quite serious. His regular non-completion of homework baffled his teachers because he was generally a high achieving and well behaved student. Interviews with his head of year revealed a lack of awareness about his home circumstances: 'I don't know where Shane lives. Does he live in a house?'

As students progressed through Key Stage 3, their attitude towards homework became more relaxed. They said that less work was set and their parents agreed. Some parents wondered how their children managed to keep up as they had not seen them engaged in homework in the evenings. Monitoring systems which required parents to sign their children's planner or homework diary were not rigorously followed up because teachers were not always sure whether parents were literate. Non-completion of homework met with different responses. In a few cases, expectations were low and, according to the students, there was no consequence. Some teachers allowed an extension on the deadline but more commonly a lunchtime detention was used as the sanction.

Vocational Courses

Government intentions to extend vocational opportunities for students in the 14-19 age range were welcomed by schools and parents but for this cohort of students the options remained limited, as initiatives would take some time to come on stream. Schools with high academic aspirations, such as the one that David attended, did not anticipate much development in this area because it would not be viable: 'It's hard to provide a [vocational] course for a small number of pupils' (head of year). Even some schools that served socially deprived areas were not in a position to offer vocational options to students, unless they were considered to be at risk of exclusion. Joe had heard about a college package that some students accessed at his school and was determined that he was going to follow that route. However, staff interviews revealed that this option was only available for disaffected students or those at risk of exclusion.

Kizzy's school, on the other hand, offered a range of GNVQs and college options but made clear that students like Kizzy (who were likely to do well in GCSEs) would be steered away from this opportunity because of the pressure of league tables, even though the benefits of a vocational route for the student might outweigh this.

> ...given obviously the pressure on the league tables and everything, they wouldn't offer that to somebody like Kizzy (head of year).

The only students destined to access a vocational package in Key Stage 4 were Dean (who had specific learning difficulties and attended a special school), Chelsea, who was hoping to spend one day a week at college to learn hairdressing and Kieran, who was due to spend two days at college and three days at school from the beginning of Year 10. His mother hoped that this would encourage him to stay on at college when he reaches 16 'to learn a trade properly'. A number of teachers believed that greater flexibility was needed in the latter part of Key Stage 3 because too many students were already becoming disaffected. One TES teacher described how it saddened him to see students who were so bright and enthusiastic in Year 6 being turned off education after nine months in secondary school. Until more flexibility is built into the Key Stage 3 curriculum, Traveller students may continue to question the relevance of its content. Marie's description of how she made her Key Stage 4 options, illustrates how important this is:

> I chose geography because I'm good at it and I chose GNVQ in ICT because everything in the future is going to be computers isn't it! Even if you work in a shop, you've gotta know how to work a computer. For DT I'm doing textiles. I chose textiles because I want to learn how to make clothes, seat covers, cushions things like that. 'Cos that's something you'll need later on. I really wanted to take Geography and Art but I don't think Art is really going to get me anywhere. Not because I'm not good at Art but its all abstract and I don't like abstract art.

Oaks and Willows

Senior teachers and school managers were asked whether there had been a need to review or adjust school rules and policies in the light of their experience with Traveller students. To return to the analogy of Oaks and Willows, it is interesting to compare these contrasting standpoints as expressed by headteachers in the study (see box on page 00).

The former statement suggests a rather unyielding (Oak) approach whereas the latter presents a more flexible and receptive (Willow) response.

The hidden curriculum of a school (including teacher attitudes) can shape unequal educational opportunities (Myers and Grosvenor 2001). Responses from teachers occasionally revealed attitudes, expectations and perceptions about Traveller students which were grounded in the deficit theory of cultural deprivation. One or two

> It is a question of them [Traveller students] getting used to the sort of regimented order and discipline that we have to have in schools. If you start having one system for the Travellers and one system for the pupils in school, you are on a loser and they must conform within certain guidelines (headteacher).
>
> In my experience, and I have met Travellers in different areas outside school, they're able to follow rules like anybody else. It just depends on the rule. If a rule's a sensible rule, that's fair enough but if it's not, they'll argue about it. Most people will! No, I think you have to interpret the rules flexibly with any individual kid, whether it be Traveller or not because kids react differently and kids have different levels of understanding and again, it's not specific to Traveller pupils (headteacher).

individuals implied that Traveller students lacked social skills and needed help to fit into the school's cultural norms. 'They needed to be nursed along ... persuaded to conform.' One senior teacher expressed the view that Traveller children may be better off having their own segregated provision, with specialist teachers, until they were ready to be assimilated into mainstream education. Another was adamant that 'They will behave and act like any other pupil in the school!'.

By contrast, other respondents expressed the conviction that all students had different needs and therefore different responses were appropriate. One headteacher maintained that if schools 'got it right for children in general, they would have it right for Travellers'. These headteachers spoke about treating students as individuals with diverse needs but emphasised high expectations for all students and acknowledged that the balance could be difficult to achieve. The view was that open dialogue and clarity were paramount in order to gain the trust of Traveller parents. If schools made exceptions for Traveller students in an attempt to avoid possible confrontation with parents, this could effectively set them apart and reinforce negative attitudes held by teachers, non-Traveller students and their parents. One mother, who recognised that the (primary) school had got the balance right, put it this way:

> Even though they respect the Traveller's way, it's still a school. [The deputy head] kept all channels open but let the Travellers know he wasn't a complete walk over!

Points for reflection

• Targeted support and centralised funding systems have historically circumvented Traveller students who are seen as being 'settled'. Do we, as this research suggests, need to consider a wider range of variables in order to understand why so many Traveller students present with poor attendance patterns during their first three years in secondary school, (whether they are settled or not), in order to prioritise support?

• Where poor attendance is due to psycho-social stress there are no quick fix solutions. Token or tangible incentives are unlikely to be effective and punitive measures may result in withdrawal from the system. Perhaps a counselling or mentoring approach may help to find and address the underlying cause? Dedicated (and preferably trained) mentors for vulnerable attendees, as suggested by the Audit Commission (1996) may be a way forward and is perhaps something that schools and TESs could build into their provision?

• Could an ecosystemic approach to addressing poor attendance help to address the issue and improve communication and understanding between schools, parents, LEAs and TESs? (In other words, examining non-attendance from the perspective of all those involved and with a consideration of how these perspectives are interrelated).

• Good quality teaching and effective support systems within school are key factors that Ofsted (2001) has identified in relation to improving attendance and behaviour. Is there a danger that too much focus on actual monitoring procedures or cultural explanations can divert attention away from the school factors that might be responsible for students' non-attendance in the first place?

• Schools, TESs and Education Welfare Services all have a role in monitoring attendance, but are all parties clear about who intervenes and when? What could be done to clarify these roles and responsibilities?

• Low expectations about attendance can become self-fulfilling. The desire to make allowances for Traveller students and their culture may be well intentioned but can result in low expectations and stereotyped assumptions. How can this be overcome?

- What more can be done to ensure that Traveller students get their entitlement to external support agencies?

4

Cultural mediators? The role of Traveller Education Services

This chapter explores and analyses the role of Traveller Education Services (TESs) and the extent to which they can impact on Traveller students' accessing school in the primary and secondary phases.

Traveller children's access to achievement in the school system may be partly attributed to the establishment of dedicated TESs within LEAs. Most TESs employ peripatetic teachers, learning support assistants (LSAs) and fieldworkers (Ofsted, 1996), who work in schools and the community to promote mainstream education and to increase attendance and attainment at school. The peripatetic flexible nature of the teachers' work means that they can respond to the needs of students and school staff within the LEA. They are also likely to be involved in issues relating to accommodation, and the health and welfare of students and their families, as all these factors affect a child's ability to access education.

Ofsted (1996) found that Traveller students' response to school was largely dependent on feeling accepted by the other students and school staff. They did best in schools which actively acknowledged cultural diversity and openly valued the Traveller experience within the school environment. Ofsted pointed out the crucial role played by the TES in this process:

> Many schools have been significantly helped in this process by the work of the TES which have provided skills, information and resources to facilitate the sensitive inclusion of the different cultures and minority ethnic backgrounds which make up the Travelling communities (Ofsted, 1996).

Thus, the role of the TES in raising awareness of Traveller cultures within school is as important for non-Traveller students and school staff as it is for the Traveller student. The TES can be seen as cultural mediators within schools, permeating the cultural boundaries and enabling access to the school system, whilst promoting a positive portrayal of Traveller cultures in the school environment. It is important, however, to acknowledge that institutions such as TESs can 'remain ethnocentric despite proclaimed ideals of tolerance' (Acton, 1974), particularly when there are relatively few Traveller TES staff. This 'piggy in the middle' role may also lead to conflict and tensions between the TES, schools and families. This issue is explored later on in this chapter.

What do TESs do?

A total of 14 TES teams were involved in the study, covering 16 LEAs: six county LEAs, five new regional authorities, three new city LEAs and two metropolitan authorities. The numbers of staff employed in TESs ranged enormously, as did the geographical areas covered, which inevitably had an effect on the level of support available within individual LEAs. The funding of TESs also affected the support available. In 1990, a new central funding arrangement gave local education authorities the opportunity to bid for a specific grant aimed at 'ensuring unhindered access to, and full integration [of Traveller children] in mainstream education' (DES, Circular 10/90, 1990). Since then, the number of Traveller Education Services across England has risen steadily and in 1998 a total of 93 LEAs, some in consortia, provided additional support for some 17,454 Traveller students in more than 3,400 schools. The total number of Traveller children in England has been estimated at around 50,000 (Ofsted, 1996).

In April 2000 the Ethnic Minority Achievement and Traveller Grant (EMTAG) replaced this funding mechanism. Within the formula, costs related to provision for Traveller students, could be held back centrally by LEAs unless there were 'sufficient' numbers of Travellers in any one school and then funds could be devolved to schools. In practice, the work of TESs 'continued in much the same way ... albeit in some at a reduced level, but in most cases with the benefit of much closer working with EMAG[1] teams' (Ofsted, 2001). In April 2001 Traveller education was 'uncoupled from EMAG and has no further requirement to devolve money to schools' (Currie and Danaher, 2001) and a separate specific grant for Traveller education was reintroduced in the shape of the Traveller Achievement Grant. More recently, the Vulnerable Children Grant was introduced with the aim of securing improved access to education for all children considered to be at particular risk of education and social exclusion. This may include Traveller children.

The study also revealed wide variation in practice in terms of TES roles and responsibilities, e.g. some services had post holders with specific responsibilities for home liaison, some did not support students in school, and some kept a watching brief only.

In addition to the attendance issues already mentioned, some of the main roles and responsibilities carried out by the TES in the study included:

• home-school liaison, including advocacy

• in-school support for students and staff including in-class support, pastoral support and advisory work

• curriculum-focused support including the provision of resources and curriculum development and modification.

These will now be considered in turn:

Home-school liaison

Most TES teams in the study were seen as having long standing and trusting relationships with Traveller parents, which sometimes extended far beyond their teaching role. Carly's mum explained: 'He isn't just a teacher to us, he's a very good friend'. This trusting relationship can be seen as particularly important when Traveller students moved into new environments and contexts, notably secondary school, with which their parents were unfamiliar. TES staff were able to offer reassurance, practical advice and support. The

TES role in home-school liaison was widely seen as vital in ensuring and maintaining Traveller students' access to mainstream education.

> It's [TES support] vital because there are times when these children feel as though the world's against them. And the beauty of the Travellers' Team is that they've all been in post some time and they tend to have known these kids since they were little and even since they were babies, so they're friends, they're not just teachers and the children and their parents trust them (secondary school SENCO).

Some schools felt that because of this trusting relationship the TES were better at communicating certain issues to parents or supporting parents and schools at times of potential conflict:

> [Name of TES teacher] is great she is a really good liaison person because the Traveller community trusts her. So if we have to say some hard things sometimes it is good that she can be in on these meetings (primary headteacher).

TES support was seen as important in providing extra background information about students and a crucial link with home: 'it would be much harder for the school to make contact without it' (primary headteacher). One TES employed post holders with specific responsibility for 'home-school liaison', who focused on issues such as attendance: 'if there is an issue with attendance the Home School Liaison officer will pick that up too' (primary headteacher) and a range of other issues, such as sex education and school trips. In all the other teams, TES teachers had responsibility for home-school liaison, and in some areas this was viewed as their primary role: 'It's a lot of liaison with the families and trying to build up the trust and the links, that's what a lot of our time is spent doing home visits and things like this' (TES support worker).

TES staff also conveyed messages and concerns to and from school when parents did not feel confident to approach the school directly or when the school felt it would be more appropriate for someone who knew the family well to deal with particular issues. For example, parents asked TES staff to relay to schools their concerns about the completion of homework set, to request additional learning support for their children, or to obtain permission to have time off school to attend culturally significant events. TES staff were also able to mediate between home and school in the context of cultural expectations concerning student/teacher relationships. This could be a potential source of conflict for some Traveller students, particularly at secondary level (as described in Chapter 5).

The role in home-school liaison played by TES support workers was viewed as particularly important for those parents with literacy difficulties. A number of parents were unable to read so TES staff were seen as an invaluable link, in terms of communication and information exchange, by both schools and parents. TES staff were also a key link with home for students whilst they were in school, as a secondary school SENCO observed:

> They will come to me and say 'can you ring [name of TES teacher]?' They want me to put them in touch ... It might be about a home matter and that's where the link comes in, it's sometimes not a school problem, and I think the children know that it doesn't matter to get help from the Travellers Education Team they just have to ask and someone will get back to them as soon as possible and listen.

TES staff were also involved in monitoring Traveller students' attendance and a number of TESs had appointed their own specialist EWOs, thus clearly delineating the role of 'support' teacher and that of the EWO who may have a possible enforcement role regarding non-school attendance. Bhopal *et al* (2000) found that 'appropriately trained and specialist EWOs can enhance access and attendance for Traveller pupils'. Certainly there was support for such roles within the TES and within schools. Although, as already discussed in Chapter 3, lack of clarity regarding who was responsible for monitoring Traveller students' attendance could mean that lapses in attendance were not addressed sufficiently swiftly or adequately. TES staff as 'cultural mediators' also helped families to access school transport and provided assistance with school uniforms in order to ease access to and regular attendance at school.

There was, perhaps, an over-reliance on the TES for home-school liaison. In some instances TES staff felt that schools should be developing closer and more direct relationships with parents. This is discussed later. However, many families and schools were communicating directly with one another and the TES were either not involved at all: 'the home school relationship is wonderful and doesn't involve me', or would only be involved in serious matters, or specific issues. One TES teacher noted that his role in home-school liaison was very much dependent on individual families:

> Mum manages the relationship with school herself [but] she will call on me for matters like uniform and she involved me the minute this question of bullying arose ... and I went up to the school with her. With [name of student] it is about the opposite I am involved right down the line ... I do a lot of negotiating between the home and school.

TES staff also played an important advocacy role in supporting parents with appeals. This ensured that children were admitted to their chosen schools. They also accompanied or took parents to SEN review meetings and other meetings regarding non-attendance, behaviour and exclusion. As Carly's mother said: '[TES teacher] was good, he took me to meetings and everything'. Some TES staff accessed additional support for students from external agencies, such as speech therapy and educational psychologists, and had been involved in the statementing process and with liaising with parents about this.

In-school support

TES staff also provided in-school support for students and staff, including in-class and pastoral support and advisory work (including INSET). Providing general in-class support for students was seen as a way of not singling out Traveller students, whilst simultaneously being available to provide support if it was needed. In addition, using this approach TES staff were also available to provide support for other students in the class and teaching staff:

> [TES role] supporting the child, but also supporting the member of staff with other children around. She is very conscious that particularly for younger boys, they don't want her sitting next to them and helping and them being identified as different but are quite happy for her to be there if she is working with a group (secondary deputy headteacher).

Traveller adults were employed as LSAs in three LEAs, which was seen as having a positive impact on Traveller students' self-esteem and confidence within schools. By providing general support, TES staff were seen by some schools as 'an integral part of our staff, which is what we'd want' (primary deputy headteacher), rather than as an 'add-on'. However, some schools noted concern regarding the seemingly 'ad hoc' nature of TES support. TES staff in-school support also included work with homework clubs, either supporting existing [school] provision for all students, or establishing lunchtime clubs for Travellers and, in one instance, their friends. Two TESs had also established on-site homework clubs to support students, recognising the difficulties some youngsters had in completing homework at home.

The relationships between TES staff and school staff and the support they were able to offer them was also seen to impact on the relationship school staff had with Traveller students:

> [Before] school staff were suspicious of the motives of the TES and the TES seemed to operate in a vacuum ... [Now there's] ... great trust between TES and school, which has meant that the suspicion of Traveller children, which was apparent amongst the staff, is now not so (primary headteacher).

Other support for school staff included joint reviews concerning students' progress, information exchange and the monitoring of attendance.

TES staff also provided focused in-class support for individual students. Nearly two-fifths (17) of the student sample had received some in-class support from the TES in Year 6 (including transition work), and just over two-fifths (18) received some in-class support at secondary school. The latter included short-term support, for example, 'settling-in' support for Bridget at the beginning of Year 7, and support for Shane in Year 7, as a way of monitoring bullying and homework issues. TES support at secondary school had a greater mentoring focus: 'I see my role as more of a pastoral support person' (TES teacher). Pastoral support and mentoring was another key focus of TESs' work, particularly at secondary school. This was incorporated into general support provided to Traveller students both in and out of the classroom: 'It is good that he comes in because it's someone Travellers can talk to, he understands' (Shelley). TES staff also provided both pastoral and academic support for specific students including those continuing into Key Stage 4 and students like Linda returning to, or starting, school in Year 9 or above. Schools viewed TES in-class support as particularly important for some students to raise their confidence and self-esteem. In Year 7

Crystal had requested support from the TES: 'it is important that she knows the support is there (head of year).

TES staff were aware of their limitations in terms of the support they could provide for 'vulnerable' students such as those at risk of exclusion. They expressed frustration at the lack of additional support available for them. For example, Kenny received TES support because he was 'at risk of permanent exclusion'. However, the TES teacher was only able to support him for an hour a week and 'all the incidents occur when I'm not there ... he needs behaviour support [but] I have never seen them do anything yet'. This highlights the need for students like Kenny to have someone to go into school for support at times of difficulty. There was a clear expectation amongst TES staff that support for students' special educational needs should be the responsibility of the school but at times this delineation of roles becomes blurred – an issue explored later in this chapter:

> We don't provide any additional support for Leanne's special educational needs which is provided by the school. I have to be quite clear about my role otherwise we tend to get swallowed up ... there's a fine line between not wanting to segregate Traveller pupils and trying to raise their achievement.

The TESs crucial involvement in transition support has already been explored in Chapter 2. TES staff were also involved in supporting Traveller students' transfer to new schools during the secondary phase.

A number of students received no TES support in school, although some TESs retained a monitoring brief over these students. Over a third (16/44) of the sample did not receive any in-school support in Year 6, whilst just under a third (11/38) did not receive any in-school support in secondary school. Some TESs were just not in a position to provide in-school support:

> We don't give any support from the team, that's the schools' responsibility ... it's a very small team so we can't offer support ... well we do for children settling into school, but long-term we can't do that because there aren't enough of us (TES teacher).

The support available was also dependent on the number of staff within the service:

> If the school doesn't shout I'm assuming all's well, I don't want to go interfering where there's no need ... it's the people that shout the loudest that get your attention when you're the only person in a vast area (TES teacher).

This TES had no secondary worker in the team. At least two other TESs were in a similar position, with all the teachers primary quali-fied, which impacted on the type of TES support available to students at the secondary level. Other TESs did not provide in-school support at the secondary level because Traveller students 'don't want us in there supporting them because it labels them' (TES teacher).

In addition to providing support for teachers in the classroom, most TESs also offered INSET to schools and those who did not felt that it would be a useful development, particularly with secondary school staff. In one LEA TES staff were also providing training to student teachers. The extent to which schools accessed the INSET available was extremely variable, with staff from a number of TESs saying that their offers of training had not been taken up by schools, or 'we put on INSET and hardly anyone turns up – those who do are not the ones you need to reach' (TES teacher). One headteacher had con-sidered linking staff participation in INSET to performance related pay to encourage staff to attend. Nevertheless, in one secondary school a TES workshop with staff had led to the production of a booklet for school staff on issues relating to Traveller education. Getting 'Traveller education' on the INSET agenda was problematic, particularly at secondary schools, where there were likely to be very few Traveller students on roll. INSET was not viewed as a priority but, as a TES teacher observed:

> When you've got one child at a school probably all the more reason to have it [INSET] than when you've got a whole load of kids, from our point of view. But from their [the school's] point of view they'll say 'oh well we've only got one [Traveller student] it's not a problem'.

Other TES staff felt that schools would not 'do anything in relation to Travellers without our service really pushing it' and that, in one school, they had only been asked to provide INSET prior to an Ofsted inspection: 'pre-Ofsted I was suddenly flavour of the month ... the minute Ofsted's over they revert to exactly where they were'.

The reaction to INSET by school staff was mixed, and in some instances quite negative. One primary headteacher felt that it 'was a bit of an imposition' and a TES teacher observed: 'when I've done INSET, I think there's almost a sneering resentment from the staff'.

Curriculum-focused support

TESs provided culturally relevant resources such as books and artefacts to schools. The majority of resources available tended to be primary-focused, reflecting the numbers of students at that level. As more Traveller students access secondary school the development of additional culturally relevant resources for this age group would be useful, although there may be sensitivities around this issue, discussed in the next chapter.

TES staff were also involved in curriculum development work at both primary and secondary levels, although there was more involvement at primary. Areas where TESs were involved in curriculum development at secondary level were PHSE and distance learning[2]. Curriculum-focused work was seen by the TES as a key area for development in a number of schools. At the secondary level, in particular, TES staff were involved in curriculum modification, such as negotiating restricted and part-time timetables, and setting up extended work experience placements.

One TES who had experienced consistent non-transfer to secondary school set up an alternative education initiative as a strategy for gradually integrating students into the secondary school. This initiative ran for two years, but most of the students attending did not transfer to secondary school. The project closed due to LEA concerns that Traveller students should be integrated into school. Nevertheless, the following September the TES had 100 per cent transfer of Traveller students to secondary school for the first time: 'whether we would have had that success if we hadn't done a bit of intermediary work with the [alternative provision] we will never know [but] I suspect it probably did help' (TES teacher). When asked whether the TES would adopt this strategy again the response was:

> No, because however much I said 'we can do this for two years' it still looked to them [Traveller parents] like I was tricking them a bit to try and get them to go to school. In some ways it was just putting off the inevitable (TES teacher).

The impact of TES support

The previous discussion has explained the importance of the TESs' role in home- school liaison as well as the support they can provide in school to both Traveller students and others, which undoubtedly helped some students operate within school. Some school staff felt that the support available from the TES had a direct impact on student's retention in secondary school, as Crystal's head of year commented:

> It is a terrific support, having someone who knows the family I think if we lost that support ... it would be very unlikely that she would continue to come to school on the basis she does.

Conversely, lack of TES support may have accounted for the difficulty in retaining some students. For example, transfer to secondary school was always going to be difficult for Seamus primarily because he was two years older than his peers. In addition he had a statement for SEN. The fact that different TES teams were supporting him in primary and secondary meant that the secondary TES did not have a relationship with the family prior to transfer which may have contributed to his non-transfer. In addition, family concerns about his transfer may not have been fully addressed. Seamus was transferring at a time when the secondary TES was in a state of flux: existing staff had retired or were not working due to illness, and a new member of staff had not yet been appointed. Greater contact with the TES may have helped Seamus transfer to secondary school and may have assisted his brother Louis' retention (he left in the Easter of Year 7). Similarly, Ronnie, Nick, Clint, Stephen and Sarah-Jane came under the remit of the same TES in the secondary phase as Seamus and Louis, which meant that their in-school TES support was withdrawn at the end of the first half-term of Year 7. Subsequently, all these students stopped attending the secondary school. When the new TES teacher was appointed she integrated them back into school and the school stressed how important her role was: 'it is really important that she is here in school without her in school I don't think the children would be here' (school staff). Despite the re-availability of TES support, all these students had left by the end of Year 8, and Ronnie and Nick never really established a regular pattern of attendance. Some of these students had needs which meant they would have difficulty operating within the secondary school environment, even with support, such as a history of poor school attendance (Ronnie and Nick), low attainment (Stephen and Ronnie) and behavioural difficulties (Stephen). The above experiences clearly show that withdrawing TES support affects some Traveller students' ability to access school and confirms the need for sustained and continuous support.

To what extent did TES involvement determine whether or not students transferred?

The TES role in supporting transfer to secondary school has already been explored in Chapter 2. The six students who did not transfer to secondary school all had some form of TES support or contact in Year 6, although only Louisa fitted the criteria for academic in-class support. So, for these students, TES involvement was not enough to make them transfer. Samantha's TES support worker thought that she had a 'good relationship' with the family until Samantha did not transfer and then her mum became 'bristly and unapproachable'. The parents of those students who were still attending in Year 9 were asked whether their child would have transferred without the involvement of the TES. The fact that they were still in school in Year 9 shows their commitment to secondary education. Unsurprisingly, of the 17 parents who responded, the vast majority (13) said their children would have transferred without the involvement of the TES. Nevertheless, three parents said that their children would not have transferred and one was not sure. For Crystal, the involvement of the TES at the point of transfer was vital. Her parents were unable to obtain a place for her at the secondary school they wanted her to attend, but the TES support teacher 'helped us get her in. If she'd had to go to another school she wouldn't have gone' (Crystal's mother). Clearly in some cases TES involvement did determine whether students transferred, although in others it was not a vital factor.

Did TES involvement aid retention?

The data suggest that it did, especially where students were particularly vulnerable, but what about the sample overall? Of the 20 students still attending in Year 9, just over half (11) had received some type of in-school support (however limited) from the TES during their time at secondary school: six received in-class support (academic and pastoral) and five received pastoral support. TES staff maintained a monitoring brief for the remaining nine students but provided no direct support. TES staff were also involved to varying degrees in home-school liaison with over a third (7) of the parents of the retained students. For students like Becky and Kenny, who both experienced behavioural difficulties at school, TES staff were providing crucial support to try and keep them in school, but both TES staff felt that the support they were able to provide was insufficient to meet the students' needs:

Expectations and tensions regarding the role of the TES

Having presented and explored TES roles and responsibilities, the various expectations placed on the service will now be considered. Expectations regarding what the TES did and what they were expected to do led to a number of tensions focusing on:

• the role of the TES

• the nature and amount of support

• communication and liaison

• TES/school relationships.

The role of the TES

How did schools' perceptions of the role of the TES match those of TES staff and vice versa? Schools generally wanted TESs to provide support for individual students, i.e. following up attendance, home school liaison, and in-class support. However, there was a difference between school and TES expectations about the nature of support and a lack of clarity about the role of the TES. The peripatetic nature of TES support and its needs-focused remit meant that school staff felt that the support on offer could be inconsistent. TES staff expressed frustration at schools' expectations of an unrealistic level of support from them. For example, a TES teacher described how a secondary school had expected her to teach a group of Traveller students when they were attending school on a part-time basis. The school also expected her to teach the students when they were not at school so that the register could be marked 'education elsewhere'. 'They said here's the classroom go and teach them ... I knew what my role was but it obviously wasn't clear to him [headteacher]'. This divergence in expectations resulted in the school submitting a complaint to the LEA:

> We have got our roles and responsibilities but I don't think they're clear to schools, so they just say 'I want this' and if you don't give it they complain.

This view was supported by Ofsted (2001) which found that 'some schools are too dependent on Traveller Education Services and do not do enough to consolidate provision for their pupils from Traveller families'. As a consequence of this, some TES staff suggested that their role involved too much crisis management; they were a reactive rather than proactive service:

> I would like to not have to be quite so responsive to how schools' perceive their needs to be. So more work preparing schools to do the work themselves. At the moment a lot of the work is very knee jerk – the school gets some kids, can't cope, we go in and sometimes that continues and the schools see us as something they need to prop them up all the time instead of doing it themselves.

TES staff felt that schools were using them inappropriately as 'fire fighters' for crisis management, rather than taking responsibility for problems themselves. For example, in relation to behaviour management: 'They use our service to immediately remove the Travellers if there is trouble ... rather than deal with it as a school with proper policies'. A deputy headteacher from one secondary school acknowledged that, in the past, the school had used TES staff: 'To do the dirty work' and used the TES 'to get our own way over things with the Traveller kids'. This reactive role meant that TES staff felt they provided too much individual support for students, which is what schools wanted, rather than allowing the TES to help schools support the students, i.e. focusing on individual, rather than school-level, support. TES staff generally wanted to take on more of an advisory role: 'I think we are going down the road of being more advisory teachers' (TES teacher), although 'the schools want us to be SNAs [Special Needs Assistants]' (TES teacher). School staff expressed concerns about this change in role:

> We very much value the actual contact time with the student in the first instance and then the follow-up after that. I am slightly concerned that it might become more advisory than hands-on (secondary school SENCO).

The nature and amount of support

Tensions were also highlighted which focused on the nature and amount of TES support provided. Specific issues concerning 'inclusion' and 'withdrawal' were raised at primary level, in particular, in relation to the nature of TES support. Should TES staff withdraw Traveller students to provide support? Withdrawal was seen as an 'undesirable' strategy by TES and school staff, for the following reasons:

• It was viewed as a form of segregated provision: a primary headteacher observed that the school's practice of withdrawing small groups of students with learning difficulties, including Traveller students, had led to 'some tensions with the TES who perceived it as segregated provision'

• It made Traveller students appear 'different': '[Withdrawal was] pandering to his [Traveller student's] self-centredness, confirming a self-image that doesn't help him within the school context ... he can easily fall back on the stereotype 'I'm different, don't tell me what to do' (primary teacher)

• It led to a concentration of resources and a consequent dilution of support, which was seen as unfair to teachers: 'The TES would withdraw a child for half an hour leaving the class teacher with 33 kids and there was a lot of jealousy and suspicion ...' (primary headteacher).

Nevertheless, withdrawal was also seen as beneficial when it provided specific pastoral support or intensive academic support. As Louisa observed: 'I look forward to that time – time when I can talk to them ... I prefer to have time out of lessons'. A TES teacher also expressed mixed views on the issue of withdrawal:

> Still pupils are having difficulty accessing the curriculum. At least if we withdraw we can get some targeted work completed, but then it's which lessons do you withdraw from and the effects on the rest of the timetable.

In-class, school-focused support, rather than withdrawal, was generally favoured by both school and TES staff:

> I find that working with her in a classroom environment is better than withdrawing because I'm often working with her

and with two or three others in the group so it works well and they see it as another teacher which is also a benefit (TES teacher).

One secondary school interviewee felt that even in-class support from the TES was problematic:

[It is] divisive and causes the children problems ... segregating them in a way they don't need segregating ... I have found that pupils are better behaved when the support person isn't there ... I think if you deal with the social issues the academic issues will ease (form tutor).

Interviewees also raised issues concerning the amount of TES support available to schools. TES staff felt that schools were using their service inappropriately and that if their support was used in a more appropriate way, such as targeted short-term intervention or in an advisory capacity, tensions relating to the lack of support provided might be alleviated. Constraints on TES resources meant that services had to prioritise support to the most needy students, which inevitably led to tensions with schools and parents:

When I saw how behind he was in his learning I asked for support but it was refused from the TES because he is settled on a site ... we thought it was terrible that he was expected to cope without additional support from that service (class teacher).

Similarly, Ben's mum expressed frustration at the lack of support available because the family were settled on a site: 'my sister's children travel around a lot and they seem to get all the help they need, when you are permanent you seem to get far less'. This illustrates the complexities involved in the provision of TES support and the legacy of a funding system that circumvented Travellers who had been settled for more than two years (DES, 1990).

A number of primary and secondary schools felt that there was insufficient support from the TES for the number of Traveller students in the school, particularly those primary schools with relatively large percentages of Traveller students. Schools were critical of the support offered such as one-to-one support, and its seemingly 'ad hoc' nature:

My teachers are dealing with 30 plus kids and the Traveller pupils. And the TES are saying they can only take one

[Traveller student] at a time ... We've taken more than our fair share. [They're] a drain on resources, we haven't sufficient support from the TES – we need continuity not drop-in visits – they should be part of the main staff (primary headteacher).

Communication and liaison

Tensions also arose around communication and liaison; interviewees cited examples of communication problems:

* between TESs and schools

* within schools

* between schools, TESs and families.

The TES played an important role in home-school liaison although TES staff felt that schools should be approaching families directly and building up relationships themselves. This, at times, led to problems about the role of the TES in home-school liaison:

I feel the schools see the children as being our responsibility and you get ludicrous things like the school phoning us to phone up the parents to arrange a hearing appointment (TES teacher).

This teacher felt there was a clear need for schools: 'to realise those children are their issue and not ours and make the parents realise that [as well]'. She also felt that parents had to take responsibility for the education of their children, that the TES could help, but ultimately it was the parents' responsibility. She maintained that the children of those parents who did take responsibility performed better at school.

TES staff also expressed frustration at the negative messages they were expected to convey to parents: 'One of the problems I've got is that contact tends to be negative and I would like more positive contact with those that are doing well' (TES teacher). Parents supported this view, saying that schools rarely contacted them to inform them about the good things that happened at school. There is a need for more positive contact with home when students are doing well, especially at secondary level because this is such a new experience for many Traveller parents. Positive liaison and communication may provide important links with parents in a non-conflictual context and boost parents' confidence about contacting schools directly.

Communication problems between TESs and schools adversely affected Traveller students' ability to access mainstream education, particularly at secondary school. Examples of lack of, or poor communication included:

- Secondary schools not being informed that TES support was to be withdrawn

- TES staff not being informed of the exclusion (fixed-term and permanent) of Traveller students: 'There are only four Travellers in the school and all except one had had some exclusions and we'd not been told about them' (TES teacher)

- TES staff not being informed of timetabling changes

- TES staff not being informed of lapses in attendance: 'Had we been aware of his attendance pattern we might have been able to intervene or support the family ... if we had closer contact with the school we could have been a bit more proactive' (TES teacher).

Communication problems within schools also meant that school staff were sometimes unaware of important information such as students' participation in sex education lessons, parents' lack of literacy, or the existence of part-time timetables for Traveller students. This resulted in a range of difficulties including tensions with parents, misunderstandings about behaviour sanctions imposed, and staff challenging Traveller students about their attendance. Using the example of sex education, a TES teacher said that in one secondary school he had consulted Traveller parents to find out which students could participate in sex education and informed the school in writing but due to poor communication within the school:

> The next week, two of the kids who should not be doing it are doing it ... They fail to send letters, or they send letters to people who can't read or kids get a detention for not bringing in a note and I've been over it and over it.

The detrimental impact that a breakdown in communication between the TES, the school, and the family could have on students was highlighted in Chapter 3.

TES-School relationship

Tensions could also arise when there was a mismatch in expectations regarding the monitoring of Traveller students' attendance. For example, staff in one secondary school had been told that the TES was responsible, whereas the TES said that they were *not* monitoring Traveller students' attendance and they expected the school to alert them to attendance problems. As a result the TES were unaware that a student in the study was not attending school. There were also tensions between schools and TESs regarding expectations about Traveller students' attendance. Differing expectations meant that in one secondary school TES staff thought that an attendance rate of 80 per cent was 'brilliant, but parents are still getting stroppy letters saying this isn't good enough'. The secondary school, on special measures had 90 per cent attendance targets to meet, but this was an LEA where previously no Traveller children had transferred to secondary school. External pressures on the school to meet targets meant that Traveller students' attendance was viewed as problematic. Other instances were given where the school felt Traveller students' attendance was acceptable but the TES did not:

> I had been told [name of student] was one of the best Travellers for attendance, now this lady comes and says: 'I don't know where you got the idea that her attendance is good' ... But I don't think her attendance is a problem ... it hasn't detracted from her work (head of year).

Most conflict arose in the TES-school relationship when TES staff challenged school actions, for example, sanctions imposed on Traveller students:

> They got rid of [name of student] in my opinion completely wrongly. They excluded him, I challenged that and got him back in, but they were gunning for him, and he was gone again within two months, permanently excluded, and they have done nothing with him since.

TES staff challenged schools' use of 'unofficial exclusions', which meant students were sent home for a few days to 'cool off'. TES staff raised this as an issue in three secondary schools in the study and in one of them this challenge resulted in the TES teacher being unable to continue working in the school.

Tensions also arose between TES and school staff in relation to per-ceived conflicts of interest. TESs' role as 'cultural mediators' meant that they felt they were often 'piggy in the middle', pressured to 'take sides' at times of conflict: 'The school sees me as 100 per cent with the Travellers and not supporting the school at all, which I'm not'. TES staff described the difficulties they faced in mediating between home and school:

> It is a tight rope ... I think mum is right at times, I think the school is right at times and I think the school is very wrong at times and I think mum gets the wrong end of the stick at times and I am in the middle (TES teacher).

TES staff also expressed frustration at schools' lack of cultural awareness, particularly in predominantly white schools, which did not address the need for support and awareness training on cultural issues because they had so few ethnic minority students. Even where TES staff managed to get INSET on the agenda, some felt that it did little to change attitudes in the school and expressed frustration at the negative impact this had on Traveller students and their families:

> It doesn't matter how much we go in there and do staff training and awareness raising – every time an incident happens we have to go in there again – it's tiring and frustrating for us so God knows what it's like for the kid and the family at the end of it (TES teacher).

This was also an issue raised by two TES staff in terms of incorporating Traveller culture into the curriculum:

> If schools are doing about multi-cultural awareness then they should be aware of Traveller culture ... It shouldn't matter if they've only got a small number of Travellers in the school, they might not have any Sikhs in the school but they still do Sikhism and Judaism, they should still do it in school (TES teacher).

Having explored the role of the TES and its attendant problems, apparent strategies which might help strengthen and develop the TES-school relationship and effective and innovative practice is already taking place.

Points for reflection

* There may be a need to ensure a clearer understanding of the TES role. This could be achieved by developing Service Level Agreements and through staff development initiatives

* Confusion over the amount and nature of TES support might also be alleviated by the school-TES support agreements

- The deployment of LSAs to support individual students may enable TES teachers to concentrate on advisory work and the support of teachers

- Regular timetabled liaison or a named person in school might help to improve communication systems between schools and TESs

- Communication between home and school could be improved by schools establishing direct relationships with families, visiting families at home and appointing a member of staff with responsibility for home-school liaison, so that TES staff are not always used as mediators, and ensuring that there is a key link person at school for parents to contact. The appointment of Traveller LSAs might also aid home-school liaison, along with the involvement of agencies such as Parent Partnership

- TES involvement in curriculum development and modification, for example, in the provision of vocational programmes and input into the Citizenship syllabus, might provide schools with useful strategies and insights

- In terms of support for Traveller students the establishment of mentoring schemes using young adult Travellers as mentors could be beneficial

- Schools' take-up of TES INSET and training can be improved by strategies such as providing more informal discussion groups within schools, including all school staff in training, consulting staff prior to training programmes and providing training for student teachers and new staff in schools.

Notes

1 Centrally funded teams whose role is to support schools in meeting the needs of Minority Ethnic pupils

2 Where schools send out schoolwork and materials for Traveller students to complete during periods of travelling.

5

They say the grass is blue: dealing with cultural dissonance

This chapter explores the concept of cultural dissonance and the impact of conflicting value and belief systems which may result from living simultaneously in two cultural worlds.

> It can be difficult [being a Traveller in school] because, like, you know one thing but then they [non-Travellers] try and teach you another. It's like, when you grow up, you learn that the grass is green don't you! But then you gradually find out that other people say the grass is blue and then they try to teach you that the grass isn't green at all, it is actually blue! And you kind of know deep down that it really isn't, it's green but no one else seems to agree (Marie).

When 13-year-old Marie made this thoughtful observation during the course of the interviews in Year 9, she was beginning to reveal how cross-cultural influences were affecting and shaping her identity. Discussion about Traveller children's engagement with secondary education often makes reference to cultural dissonance (for example Hawes and Perez, 1995; Jordan, 1996). Hancock (2000) suggests that too much formal learning is considered to be a threat to the Romani way of life. Thus, the longer the period of schooling, the greater the likelihood that young Travellers will yield to the influences of the majority culture. Clay (1999) postulates that the values of predominately white, middle-class teachers and in-creased opportunities to mix with members of the opposite sex and with non-Traveller peers represent pervasive forces which threaten to attract young Travellers away from their own community and traditional way of life. As Traveller children move through the education system, they are increasingly exposed to the norms and values of the majority culture and the influence of peers as 'signi-ficant others'.

It is likely, therefore, that the impact of culture-based role demands and the need for young Traveller students to manage the often con-flicting expectations of their families and community on the one hand, and their teachers and non-Traveller peers on the other, is most apparent when Traveller students progress to secondary school. The 'blue grass' analogy Marie provides illustrates the complexity of re-conciling cultural dissonance. She goes on to describe how identi-fication with two cultures is developed:

> Or it's like, say if you went to live in France for a couple of years. When you're round everyone else and you hear the way they're talking, you can pick up all the different words and you pick up the language and you gradually fit in and it's like that at school. But then, when you come home, it's all different again and you can be yourself.

Marie's mother also described how she tried to ensure that her chil-dren adapted to both cultures: 'so that they have two choices at the end of the day. They know the Traveller way of life, but then they know the other ways in case they want to go into a house and be settled'.

Cultural identity

In order to explore the students' perceptions of their cultural identity, the research team asked all sets of participants whether they thought the teachers and other students at the secondary schools, *knew* that the children were Travellers, and, if so, *how* did they know? The students and parents were also asked whether they thought it was a good thing to have other Traveller students in the school and why. Their use of Romani language was explored and the children and their parents were asked to consider levels of cultural awareness in their schools and whether there was anything they would like teachers and students to know about the Gypsy Traveller culture. These questions were designed to explore aspects of the students' own sense of identity, their configuration of loyalties and experiences of identity disclosure.

Data including the number and spread of other Traveller students at each secondary school were provided by Traveller Education Services at the beginning of the project, although one TES was unable to provide this information, as it did not keep records of that kind. From these data, it was ascertained that 28 of the 38 students transferred to schools with nine or fewer Traveller students in the school. A quarter of the students (9) transferred to secondary schools in which they were the only Traveller student in their year group and, in four of these cases, there were no other identified Traveller students anywhere on the school roll. Of these nine students, seven completed Key Stage 3. Louis and Peter both left before Year 8.

Ten students attended schools which had ten or more Traveller students in total, including one school with more than thirty Travellers on roll. Of these ten, four boys left before the end of Key Stage 3. Of the remaining six, one transferred to a special school, another moved to a different area and changed schools and four were still attending the same school by the end of Key Stage 3. These data show no apparent link between likelihood of retention and the number of other Traveller students on roll. However, of those students that did complete Key Stage 3, seven (more than one in three) had transferred to schools where they were the only Traveller student in their year group. This and other variables are examined in more depth in Chapter 8.

During the interviews the students were asked whether there were any other Traveller students in their school, with a follow-up question to elicit their views on this. Half of the students interviewed felt that it was good to have other Traveller students in the same school. The reasons they provided were often related to social, emotional and even physical security:

> Yes, because when some of me mates aren't at school I can just play with them [other Travellers] (Kenny).

> I'd like it if there were more Travellers in school 'cos it'd be more people to hang around with (Kimberly).

> I think it's a good thing. I don't know why really ... it just is. To have something in common with other kids (Shelley).

> It's better when there are other Travellers 'cos if anything happens you know that someone else is there with you (Sarah-Jane).

Nine parents thought that it was better for their children to be in a school with other Travellers for reasons of social and emotional security and five believed that schools with a tradition of having Traveller students were more likely to be aware of cultural considerations. Interviews with parents also identified a strong pressure on Traveller students to protect or 'look out for' their younger siblings and cousins in school. Parents who had older children already at secondary school often appeared reassured that younger siblings would be taken care of and expressed less anxiety. Students themselves also recognised the benefits of this: 'It helps having Teresa there. She sticks up for me'. Interviews with teachers suggested that older siblings would sometimes take responsibility for reporting instances of bullying or racial harassment or would take matters into their own hands and deal with the perpetrator directly (see Chapter 6).

However, these perceived advantages (of having other Traveller students in school), were tempered with concerns about stereotyped behaviour and racist attitudes which might prevail. Thirteen mothers and eight students pointed out the potential disadvantages. For example:

> It depends who they are and where the school is. Because if it's a school with lots of other Travellers then you'll fit in quite well but then, if they have all got a bad name, then the people who aren't Travellers won't like you (Shane, Year 9).

> I think it helps if there are a few others [Traveller students] but if you get too many, you might get some naughty ones and then the teachers just lump you all together and you get the blame for everything (Charlie, Year 6).

> The boys just get us [Travellers] all into trouble! They are rude. Fred was excluded because he kept making trouble. I think things have got better since they went (Bridget, Year 6).

The mothers expressed similar views and felt that the presence of other Travellers in school could have a detrimental effect on their children's education.

> I think that the teachers do tend to treat all the Travellers the same. You know, if they are fighting, they pull our kids off first. So I don't think it helps them really – going to a school where there's a lot of Travellers.

> I would rather my kids went to a school where there weren't other Travellers to be honest ... they all get looked on as bad news.

> No, it doesn't help when there are loads of Gypsy children. They can't get enough help.

Those children who transferred to secondary schools where there were already several other Traveller students, or where there was an established pattern of having Traveller students on roll, appeared to be more relaxed about whether or not people knew they were Travellers. Most of the students in the study, however, transferred to secondary schools where there were few other Traveller students and were therefore culturally isolated. Thirty-two students (84 per cent of the sample) transferred to secondary schools where there were less than five other Traveller students in their year group.

'Passing'

> I think people who are ashamed of being Travellers is very bad people. 'Cos they're hiding who they are. It's like Indians who try to be like they are white. It's like that. You are trying to hide who you really are. And I tell people that I'm a Traveller and I tell them 'if you don't like it then lump it 'cos that's who I am' (Linda, Year 9).

> I think a lot of the Travellers don't want people to know. Which is wrong, because we stand as a race in a way. I think its wrong that they should think like that (Marie, Year 9).

Both Linda and Marie presented as articulate and confident young women who were open about their identities but both described how friends and acquaintances pretended that they were not Gypsies at school.

Where individuals adopt the strategy of hiding their ethnic or cultural identity in order to gain acceptance from members of the dominant group, it is known as 'passing' (Acton, 1974; Tajfel, 1978). According to some commentators such as Lee (1993) and Hancock (1997) this is a fairly common institutionalised response by Gypsies to deeply-rooted racism. Two girls in the sample adopted this strategy from the outset. Louisa articulated a conscious attempt to hide her ethnic identity completely in primary school 'No-one knows I'm a Traveller and that's the way I want it'. Even Louisa's best friends were unaware that she lived on a Traveller's site. Louisa, who had previously been a victim of racial bullying did not achieve secondary transfer. Kizzy lived in a house and, until her primary and secondary teachers were informed about the project, the fact that she was a Traveller wasn't known to them. 'I was just amazed when I found out' (head of year). When interviewed in Year 8, Kizzy confirmed that she had still not told anyone at school that she was a Traveller. She said that she did not want people to know. Even in Year 9, Kizzy continued to exhibit 'passing': 'No, they don't know. I never really talk about it. It's not an issue'. She did not associate with other Traveller students and said that she did not use Romani words because there was 'no point to it'. Kizzy completed Key Stage 3 and aspired to higher education. Two other girls, Chelsea and Becky began to show signs of denial of their cultural identity during Year 9:

> She'll say 'I'm not a Gypsy!' She'll go all defensive on you. 'I'm not a Gypsy. I'm the same as everybody else!' Because they pick on her that way, she don't even want to acknowledge it. 'No I'm not!'
>
> I says, ' You're at home, we know what you are'. 'No I'm not. I'm not a Gypsy, OK!' You get to the stage where you think 'I could batter you at times'. Why let someone else drum everything out? She ought to be proud. Then, other times like yesterday she says these post-16s were picking on her and she says 'If they come to my house they'd have a shock wouldn't they? They want to go home and clean their houses up, half of them, us Gypsies aren't like that'. So one minute she's not and the next minute you are and that's the way she is ... she's getting to denial 'I'm not' then all of a sudden she forgets and it's 'yeah I am' but mainly she's on the defensive (Chelsea's mother).

Becky's trust in a new friend had been betrayed when she was in Year 7:

> 'I don't trust any of them. Even me mates. Cos I told Amy something ... a secret of mine. I told her I lived in a caravan, 'cos she was going to find out sooner or later ... and she spread it around. I brought her brother to my caravan as well but he's blabbed. He's told everyone on the bus and it's got out into school! People call me 'slag'.'
>
> The family later moved into housing and as far as Becky was concerned, this act signified the detachment of her cultural identity. 'I'm not a Traveller any more, because I live in a house ... Just because I lived in a caravan and my nana lives in a caravan ... it don't mean that I'm Gyppo' (Year 9).

According to Bridget's Year 6 teacher, she had always been quite guarded about her ethnicity and when the TES teacher encouraged her to look at some Traveller resources, 'she didn't want to know'. Interviews at home revealed that her older sister was hiding her identity in secondary school. Eileen's older brother too, hid his ethnicity at secondary school. According to Eileen and her mother, he did not want Eileen to transfer to the same school in case she 'blew his cover' and he had told his friends that he lived on a nearby housing estate. In the event, Eileen did attend a different school from her brother but eventually his identity was disclosed and the predicted bullying ensued:

> He was fine there until they found out what he was and then they started bullying him. And seriously, that's why he ain't been back.
>
> Researcher: Did they not know he was a Traveller before then?
>
> No. He didn't tell 'em. And he wouldn't let me go down the school and that because he was too *shoshi*. So they didn't know. But as I say, when they found out, they all started bullying him so I took him out. He'd been there all them years so they can't have been 'friends' could they!' He got nuisance phone calls – people ringing up and saying your trailer's on fire'. Things like that. Obviously we reported it to the school but we never heard anything about it. They said 'we can't do anything because we don't know who it is' (Eileen's mother).

Eileen, Bridget and Gemma all said that in Year 7 it was only their close friends who knew that they were Travellers. While Joe was relaxed about disclosure, his younger brother also denied being a Traveller and Crystal said that her cousin hid her identity in secondary school. Apart from Louisa, Kizzy, Chelsea and Becky, none of the other students in the sample adopted this coping strategy, although some said that they disclosed gradually once trust had developed. David, for example, transferred from a primary school which celebrated Traveller culture but he hid his identity for the first few days in secondary school. David 'gradually came straight' with peers but was then subjected to unreported bullying for several weeks. Others, like Danny and Shane, said that they weighed up the risk of disclosure and sometimes chose to keep quiet. When Danny transferred, he was selective about who he disclosed his identity to and Shane kept a low profile when he moved to a different secondary school.

> When you get talking to people and they ask where you live, sometimes I tell them and they are OK, sometimes they go off you when they know and sometimes I don't bother telling them about who I really am ...'cos it's better not to (Danny, Year 8).

> I was sitting next to this girl the other day and she was saying 'I hate Travellers don't you? I said 'Not really.' And she said 'Oh I do! They stink and they're all thieves!' I said 'Not all of them are' and she said 'What do you know about it anyway?' I had a little smile to myself and thought if only she knew! I thought it was quite funny (Shane, Year 8).

All these examples provide confirmation that some Traveller students do elect to disguise their ethnicity in school. Although not explicitly stated in every case, it is likely that the motives for this behaviour are related to self-protection (from past experience of racism) and a desire for social acceptance. The nature and prevalence of racism is explored in Chapter 6.

Identity markers

By the beginning of Year 8 most students believed that their cultural identity was known generally by peers and teachers with whom they came into contact. When asked how people knew that they were Travellers, some students such as Kenny, Kimberley, Glyn, Ronnie, Clint and Kieran mentioned specific indicators such as their name or accent. Gemma described how she was watched from a distance by two older girls who eventually approached her to ask if she was a Traveller like them. According to TES data, there was only one other Traveller student at the school apart from Gemma, which suggests that one of these girls may not have disclosed her identity. Although the girls apparently had no prior knowledge of Gemma, they had sensed her ethnicity. Interestingly, Marie and a couple of the mothers who were interviewed, spoke about this instinctive recognition of other Travellers: 'No matter where you go, you can always tell another Traveller. Something just clicks'.

Association with relatives already attending was also a likely marker of identity. Eleven of the students had an older sibling on roll when they transferred and others mentioned cousins who were in school. Danny and Sarah-Jane said that their ethnicity was probably first disclosed by primary school peers who had transferred with them to the same school. In Danny's case, this was perceived to be a beneficial factor as he had been a popular student in primary school and this peer support in the induction phase helped him to gain acceptance from other students. Apart from these specific identity markers, students said that their peers found out because it just came out in conversation. 'If they ask where I live, I just tell 'em!'

Students were not so sure whether their subject teachers at school were aware of their ethnicity. Fourteen students mentioned that certain teachers treated them differently or unfairly and, of these, eight made references to maths or science teachers.

> He [science teacher] don't like Travellers. 'Cos my cousin and my mate, they have trouble with him as well and they're both Travellers ... I'm sure he's got a thing about Travellers because I made it clear from the start I was a Traveller, everybody in the class knows and some of them said 'oh keep quiet about it, don't let him know that' ... but I ain't bothered, no, I'll tell him. So he didn't like me and he didn't like Adam 'cos he associates with me and he associates with lots of Travellers and he knows half the Traveller's language and he talks it with us (Joe, Year 9).

> I don't like my maths teacher because he treats Asians and Travellers differently (Sarah-Jane, Year 7).

These perceptions and experiences are discussed in Chapter 6.

Cultural awareness

Teachers with responsibility for pastoral support, such as heads of year and form tutors, were perceived by the students to have a better awareness and understanding of their culture and background. A few students mentioned English and humanities teachers who showed greater empathy with and insight into the Traveller way of life. Shane felt that his humanities teacher had a good awareness and Marie spoke of two English teachers who showed interest and empathy. Gemma described her history teacher in this way:

> He understands about Travellers because in history there was like Jews and Travellers got killed in the gas chambers. Mr Thomas explained about getting picked on because of being slightly different, and he talked about me and about Bhavin who's coloured. He said if I don't do this no one will understand – that was OK.

She went on to say how this teacher told her that he'd driven past the place where she lived and admired her horses: 'He said it looked nice and that!' One or two other teachers built upon a shared interest in horses, to develop positive relationships with students: 'Once she and I established the horse connection, she started bringing in photos to show me'. Overall, however, the Traveller students and their parents believed quite fervently that teachers and non-Traveller peers had a limited understanding and awareness of their culture and that the wider societal stereotyped attitudes prevailed. Bridget's mother voiced her concerns in this way:

> I don't think they know very much. I would like them to understand that we're not dirty, the way they think. That we're not Travellers that throw their rubbish everywhere. Not everybody's the same. There's difference in all of us!

Stacey pointed to a lack of fundamental awareness about ethnicity and lifestyle:

> They think if you just go into a trailer you can be a Traveller. They think 'cos I live in a house now I'm not a Traveller any more. They don't understand about having to go away for weddings and things like that cos when you're away for a couple of days and you say 'I've been to the wedding'. They say 'well you only need one day off'.

Joe (Year 9) could see no point in learning French. His teacher told him that if he wanted to be a car dealer, he might need to travel to France and communicate with customers or business contacts over there. As far as Joe was concerned, this showed a complete mis-understanding: 'I ain't going to BE that sort of car dealer! It's gonna be used cars and going down the auction and that!'

Interviews in Year 6 suggested that in just over half of the primary schools (17) there were reported attempts to celebrate diversity and raise awareness through displays of resources and curriculum initiatives including assemblies, discussion work, drama, literature and humanities' projects. Of the secondary schools in the study, only five reported specific curriculum initiatives or displays of cultural resources. One of these schools had asked the TES to help set up a display prior to its Ofsted inspection. Two other schools had put up displays of books and photographic images in public areas. This prompted a mixed response from the young people concerned. While Eileen expressed some interest in a dictionary of Romani words that she came across in her school's display of books, both Shelley and Leanne said that they felt 'embarrassed' and 'shamed' by displays of Traveller images in their school. 'They've got things on the wall about Gypsies and it's all wrong!' Some images apparently showed rubbish near unofficial sites, others were antiquated 'The kids said: 'How old fashioned! Do you live in a wagon?''.

Recent DfES guidance (2003) advises all schools to have resources in classrooms and libraries which give a positive view of Traveller culture and lifestyle. However, when the students were asked what they thought the teachers and other students ought to know or under-stand about Traveller culture, almost every student said 'nothing' or 'I don't want them to know anything'. This response was almost unanimous and quite emphatic, even though many of the students had attended primary schools where their culture had been cele-brated quite openly. Some students added that they just wanted to be treated equally and fairly, not differently. The ignorance the students encountered about their cultural and social life was a source of angst and irritation, but they themselves showed no desire to address it. This is illustrated by Sarah-Jane's response:

> There's been Travellers coming to this school for a long time but they don't know what it means really. They think a Traveller means like when you're in a tent travelling up and down ... I don't tell them anything ... I don't want them to know anything.

Theories of identity (Erikson, 1968; Marcia, 1980) identify adolescence as the period when exploration of identity is at its height. Therefore it is not surprising that attempts by teachers to raise cultural awareness in secondary schools may not be welcomed by young Travellers. A similar finding was also reported by Cline *et al* (2002) and suggests that schools and Traveller Education Services may need to involve and consult actively with the young Traveller students about the way in which their culture could be reflected and valued in school. Helena, for example, had been encouraged to design a website about Traveller culture as part of an IT project. This had given her the opportunity to select and present the information in her own way. As one enlightened SENCO pointed out, the typical reliance on library displays and photographic images is at best superficial: 'It's the easy way to do Travellers'. Such an approach may present different Traveller communities as a homogenous group and obscure the central issue of the dominance of white, middle-class culture in the hidden curriculum.

Cultural traditions and the configuration of loyalties

Language

Although it is not widely known, many English Gypsy Travellers retain the use of a largely stigmatised language known as Anglo-Romani. According to Acton *et al* (2000) the language is a mixture of English and Romani (ratio 80:20), which is spoken rapidly and is therefore unintelligible to outsiders. Users of Anglo-Romani are adept at 'code switching', even between sentences.

Shared use of language can be a positive force within communities and may be used by minority groups to emphasise their distinctiveness in order to reinforce a sense of group identity. The use of Anglo-Romani by Gypsy Travellers can be seen as a positive cultural marker which may at times prove useful in countering or subverting the discrimination of the non-Traveller community. Thus, knowledge of Romani may be used to create and maintain boundaries and to reinforce the concept of a separate cultural identity. Courthiade (1993) has suggested that, even for those Travellers who do not speak Anglo-Romani, the language remains a cultural reference point and an affirmation of shared identities. Conversely, the incorporation of Romani words into the English language also reflects the level of interaction with the wider community and its culture. Although acculturation usually applies to the behaviour of the non-dominant group, it is a two-way process. For example, British youth culture reflects an eclectic mix of ethnic influences in relation to music, fashion and patterns of communication. Although Traveller culture remains largely rejected and stigmatised by the settled population, there were examples of *gauje* students adopting Romani vocabulary. Within the school environment, the knowledge that Traveller students have their own language may be a source of pride and support for Traveller children. However, there is little formal recognition in schools that Traveller children may be bi-lingual and the value of Travellers having their own language is not always acknowledged.

Bridget, Becky, Kizzy, Chelsea and Gemma all said that they did not use any Traveller or Romani words either at home or at school. This may have been a guarded response on their part. Gemma's mother later told the researcher that Romani was 'second-nature' to her daughter. Chelsea's mother confirmed that her daughter had started to claim that she didn't understand the Romani words used by family members. Chelsea, Kizzy and Becky all exhibited a weaker identification with Gypsy culture in their responses to related questions. The other students all said that they used Traveller words to some extent, although not all recognised it as being a legitimate 'language.'

> It's like a language, but it ain't a language. It's like words but some people wouldn't understand it (Kenny).

> They look at me funny and I say 'sorry' and I speak it how it should be said (Helena).

Kimberley's mother confirmed that her family spoke a Traveller language 'like Gaelic.' Being of Irish descent this was probably a reference to the use of Gammon or Cant, a language derived from Gaelic and spoken exclusively by Irish Travellers (Binchy, 2000). In the majority of cases, Romani was reportedly used at home and also in private with Traveller friends or relatives at school: 'When I'm talking to other Travellers, I always talk like that', 'it just comes natural'.

A few students, for example, Sarah-Jane, Linda, Eileen, Shane and Danny said that if a *gauje* student overheard a conversation between them and another Traveller and asked what certain words meant, they would not wish to tell them. In this way, Anglo-Romani can be used by students to deliberately exclude non-Travellers from their conversations. Language can be source of support between Traveller students, an affirmation of shared identity and also as a form of protection, allowing Traveller students to mark the cultural boundaries between themselves and others. These students may have been using language to maintain a positive ethnic boundary and provide cultural security within school. As Shain (2003) points out, this strategy can also be an effective mechanism for dealing with racism as it provides students with a sense of power over those who subject them to abuse. Eileen commented that she and her friend used Romani to insult *gaujes* without their knowledge: 'we call the children names and they go 'what?'' Linda also used this strategy in school:

> Sometimes me and my brother would speak it together when we didn't want people to understand. Like, he'd say 'I'm gonna mor [kill] that *gauje* in a minute!' (Linda).

Seven of the girls told the researchers that *gauje* students in their schools had started to adopt Romani words and terms for their own use.

> All our mates that ain't Travellers try to pick it up and start to say some of the words. They say: 'What does that mean? ... How do you say this ...?' (Leanne).

> I've learnt my mates what some of the words mean because I'm always saying them (Crystal).

Joe (who attended a school with large numbers of Travellers) was the only male student who mentioned this phenomenon in a positive way. He described how he and a few other Traveller students made a conscious effort to spread the vocabulary throughout the school.

> Me cousin and Sam have taught some of the Year 10s and there's three or four Travellers in my year and we teach all the other little kids. And they all know it now, they can all talk to us! They go round saying: 'Alright then *mush*?' 'Come on, *jel* on' and '*Kushti*'. You don't get in a proper conversation with them but they just come out with odd words in their conversation. But they do know what you're saying even if you do say it all in Traveller's [language]. Some kids are snotty about it but I'm not bothered. It's up to them what they think, innit?

The above comments show that Traveller students having their own language can be a source of pride for them and sharing that language may be seen as a way of gaining acceptance amongst their non-Traveller peers. Thus, some Traveller students saw benefits associated with letting non-Travellers have some limited insights into their cultural world.

There were one or two examples of individual teachers showing a positive interest in the use of Anglo-Romani and one TES teacher had developed a language project with the students to produce a book with Romani vocabulary. Other students, however, said that their use of language was seen by adults at school as either a form of swearing or insolence.

> The dinner lady moans when we use Traveller language (Crystal, Year 6).

> At primary school we had a supply teacher who thought I was swearing once! I was talking in Traveller's language to Michael and she thought I was swearing. I walked out of class and sat in the playground! (Shane, Year 7).

> One teacher said 'I don't like you two talking like that' (Eileen, Year 9).

> The teachers told us not to do it [use Romani] because it's not right (Linda, Year 9).

The way these experiences were reported by the students suggested an ignorance and devaluation of their culture by school staff.

Maintenance of customs

Although the parents were a little more guarded than their children in their responses to questions about the use of language, Glyn's mother was quite emphatic in her belief that Traveller parents should teach Romani to their children. She felt that it was so important because there was no literary tradition and therefore no other way of teaching it:

> It's different with Asian people because that'll be in books but not our language – yes there's little bits and pieces but not everything so we've still got to sit down and learn them ourselves for them to remember.

Other customs and traditions were maintained by parents and relatives, regardless of whether or not the students were settled in housing or on sites. Half the original sample (22) said that they had travelled with their families to traditional Gypsy fairs, although this pattern was likely to be curtailed once the children were attending secondary school. Of the twenty students who completed Key Stage 3 sixteen said that they did not travel away or go to fairs during term time. However, Marie's family had spent time in the summer holidays re-visiting traditional Traveller routes with their horses and a tent. Joe's mother told the researcher how she took her children to a Romany museum to teach them about their heritage and maintained certain customs at home, even though the family had been housed for a number of years:

> I always try to encourage mine to remember it. Keep it [the culture] alive ... I think if they lose that bit of history, they divert and then they don't know where they're going then. It's a different lifestyle but we still keep the Traveller traditions. It's like, I never wash up in a bowl. I keep all me separate bowls and things.'

Linda (Year 9) illustrated the maintenance of cultural taboo around pollution (known as *mochardi*).

> We class ourselves as very clean people but they don't. And we can walk into a house and we can be disgusted! Like, we won't have a dog or a cat in the place we live, we find that very, very disgusting. Not all *gaujes*, but some will have them all laying on their beds and all around the kitchen tops and we find that just revolting! But then, they'll say we're dirty!

Travellers' responses sometimes included a denigration of *gauje* culture and values, which, according to Clay (1999) can be used as a defence mechanism to help to establish and maintain cultural boundaries. According to cultural psychologists such as Berry *et al*

(1986) the maintenance and development of one's own culture is essential in order to avoid assimilation and cultural disintegration. However, individuals who exhibit strong associations with their own culture but weak associations with the mainstream culture are more likely to be segregated. According to Berry *et al* both these positions (assimilation and segregation) mark a loss of identity and can lead to lower levels of motivation, educational attainment and even to social deviance. This theory suggests that a secure sense of cultural identity and the potential for achievement could be attributed to a strong and positive identification with both cultures, rather than a rejection of one or other. This is not achievable if the policy and practice of the dominant society does not welcome that maintenance of cultural heritage and participation, especially when other members of the minority community are reluctant to identify with the dominant culture.

Community influences

Interviews with the mothers emphasised how relatives or Traveller neighbours sometimes questioned the logic of putting children (particularly boys) through secondary education. The assumption here was that the young people should be engaged in more meaningful activities, such as preparation for adulthood in the Traveller community.

> They used to say 'what have you got him still in school for? What is he going to learn now? There's nothing for him to learn any more. Why isn't he out with the boys learning how to get his living?' So that put a lot of pressure on me.

> He is a big old boy. He's got a moustache and everything. And all the Traveller people kept taking the piss out of him, do you know what I mean? Calling him a wimp and that. They don't take so much notice of the girls but for the boys it's different. They [extended family members] say 'they've had all them years in the school learning 'that way' they should spend their older years learning the 'Traveller way'. 'Cos when he gets a woman, he won't be able to keep her! ... My mother-in-law says: 'school's not a place for children!' (I could strangle them sometimes!).

Interviews also revealed that some students were teased by Traveller peers who were no longer in the school system. Again, this type of response was targeted at the boys rather than girls. Danny and Kieran were both taunted with shouts of 'school boy' by local Traveller youths. Similarly, Louis and Seamus were teased by other boys on the site: 'look at the boys in blazers!' and had kids banging on the side of the trailer when they were trying to do homework. Others, who said they were not teased, still thought it was unfair that cousins or other children on the site 'got away with' not having to go to school.

Overall, the mothers in the sample were determined to do what they felt was 'right' for their children, even if this meant defending their judgement and fielding criticism from family members, including their husbands. (This supports the findings from an earlier study by Littlewood (1996) which concluded that the factor most likely to influence educational take-up was the attitude of the mother.) Eight of the mothers described a gate-keeping role and claimed that they had 'battles' with their husbands who wanted the children (five girls and three boys) out of school. The fathers of the girls were worried about their moral welfare in school. These mothers were fairly dismissive and felt that their husbands were being old-fashioned. A couple of the mothers said that they had had to persuade their husbands to let their daughters go on residential trips. In a few cases, mothers appeared to be managing a delicate balancing act and admitted to withholding certain information or even lying about behavioural incidents, or extra-curricula activities, to their husbands, in case this jeopardised the continued engagement of their children in school. Of the eight cases where there were strong objections from fathers, four students completed Key Stage 3 but four students had left before the end of Year 9.

Protective behaviour and moral codes

Parents' concerns and anxieties about their children's moral, emotional and physical welfare in school were expressed throughout the study. The intensity of this protective attitude was also raised by some of the primary school teachers who generally saw this as a positive and admirable attribute. One Year 6 teacher said that the Traveller children were 'put on a pedestal of love' by their parents. In another school, the headteacher compared the Travellers' attitudes to child-rearing favourably with that of non-Traveller parents:

> I think our Travellers down there are far more caring of their children and more protective than many of the other families we've got (primary headteacher).

There was a perception amongst teachers, however, that Traveller children had more freedom (than non-Traveller children) at home and were treated more as adults and this was why some found it difficult to settle in school and accept authority. Although interviews with the students and their parents confirmed some truth in this assumption (particularly in relation to domestic and life skills), they also suggested a comparatively sheltered upbringing in other respects. The following extracts from parent interviews illustrate this:

> I know you think they're big girls [ages 13 and 15] but I've never let them out loose, you know what I mean? There's a lot of perverts about. You read so many things. I'm one of them over-protective mums!

> When my boys come home, [ages 14 and nearly 16] they don't leave this ground. I don't let them go off up the street and things like that 'cos I would rather them be where I know where they are. There will be a day when I can't stop them, they will when they are older, but I don't believe in it, letting them go on the streets and get into trouble, and I know they think I am mad, which I know they do, but I don't really care ... For us it's different. When you live in a trailer, you have your children in your sight 24 hours a day. We always know they are safe. I know it sounds like we are overprotective but you hear so many things these days.

Joe (aged 13) was allowed to drive his mother's car off-road, yet was not allowed to go shopping in town with his friends on a Saturday afternoon in case he was mugged: 'If they see little kids with money, they are going to nab that off them'. This example also demonstrates how the concepts of safety and danger can be culturally determined and may lead to cultural dissonance when children are exposed to conflicting values. Joe pleaded with his mother to let him go into town, claiming that younger boys were allowed to go. His mother explained that her rules were different to those of *gaujes*, to which he replied: 'well why do we live here [in a house] then? Why can't we live up there [on the site]?'

Traveller parents' desire to protect their children from physical or emotional harm sometimes meant that social and educational opportunities were restricted. The ultimate example of this is where parents maintained that they would not compel their children to go to school at all if they were unhappy there (this was also found by Clay, 1999).

School trips

A quarter of the children in the sample were not allowed by their parents to go on residential trips in either primary or secondary school and a few were not allowed to go on day trips to the coast, or other venues that were some distance away from home. Parents' main concerns were related to fear about children's physical safety, often supported by references to stories in the press. The following fears were mentioned:

- fear of children drowning

- insufficient supervision by staff

- children getting kidnapped

- traffic accidents – especially involving coach journeys

- bomb threats.

The students who were not allowed to go gave no indication that they wished it to be any other way. Some said that they did not want to be away from home or 'you have to do work'. Even those who said that their mum (or dad) wouldn't let them said they were not bothered by the decision.

The same number of students, however, had been allowed to take part in residential trips, including outward-bound type activities and one trip abroad. Interestingly, all but one of the children in this latter group, completed Key Stage 3.

Sex education

When parents were asked whether they had any worries or concerns about secondary school, or if there was anything they would like schools to know or realise about Traveller culture, nine mothers and one father mentioned sex education. Their main concern was that they did not want their children to learn about sex in school. Strict moral codes are a feature of Traveller culture and it is generally unacceptable to discuss sexual matters in mixed company.

> Travellers don't believe in teaching their children that, that early, at that age ... It's like a belief amongst Travellers.

> We don't want them to learn sex education. I understand they have to learn about AIDS and protection and that but he doesn't have to learn about uteruses and afterbirth! He's never going to have any!

> I don't want her thinking it's alright to buy condoms!

> We don't like them to learn sex education. That is out of the question.

> They learn filth in them big schools.

All of these parents had previously made their views known to the primary schools and, having received notification about videos or sex education lessons, had used their right to withdraw their children from these lessons. Schools' responses all reflected a willingness to respect these parental requests and the parents generally felt that schools were understanding, although, in one case, a communication breakdown in school had apparently led to some children being present in lessons from which their parents had wanted them withdrawn. Interviews with primary headteachers and Key Stage 3 teachers also revealed that although sex education was not an issue for all of their Traveller students, this type of parental response was probably more widespread than the data here indicate. Maybe these ten parents felt particularly strongly about the issue or some parents chose not to volunteer their concerns. However, of the ten students whose parents did choose to object in this way, three did not transfer to secondary school and six had left their schools before the end of Key Stage 3. These students also tended to echo their parents' attitudes to sex education. The tenth student (Crystal) did complete Key Stage 3, and even began to participate in relevant PSHE lessons in Year 9 at her own request and with her mother's permission.

Drugs

Ten of the mothers said that they worried about their children coming into contact with illegal drugs at secondary school. Worries about drugs are certainly not exclusive to Traveller parents and this is too small a sample from which to draw any conclusions about cultural dissonance.

In three cases, this factor had influenced the choice of secondary school for girls and their parents said they had made a conscious effort to avoid schools seen as having a drug problem. This suggests that their anxiety about drugs was contextual rather than general, that it related to specific schools as opposed to *gauje* society per se. Two parents acknowledged that drug problems existed in both Traveller and *gauje* communities and complained about local Traveller teenagers who hung around the site 'smoking weed and drinking.' These parents were pleased that their children were at school and away from the negative influence of these young people.

The other seven mothers said that they were worried to some extent. Some were philosophical: 'I know there are drugs out there but you just have to hope they'll be sensible' whilst others were more anxious: 'I said 'be really careful and don't take a drink or sweets off anyone' in case they had drugs put in them.

Of the ten students whose parents voiced concerns about drugs, the four girls completed Key Stage 3, whereas the six boys did not. In two cases, these were the same boys whose parents had voiced strong objections to sex education

Involvement and participation

Extra-curricula activities

A total of eighteen students (41 per cent) said that they participated in one or more school clubs or extra-curricula activities during their final year in primary school. This group included ten boys and eight girls. The activities are shown in the table below:

Table 5.1 Extra curricula involvement in Year 6

Type of club or activity	Number of students
Football	9
Other sports	8
Netball	4
Drama	3
Music	2
Religious group	1
Dancing	1

Levels of extra-curricular activity dropped slightly during Year 7, although thirteen students (36 per cent of the remaining sample) participated in a wide range of lunchtime or after-school activities. This group included a few more boys than girls, although Shelley, Leanne, Helena and Crystal attended several different clubs and activities each and were the most actively involved.

Table 5.2 Extra curricula involvement in Year 7

Type of club or activity	Number of students
Singing/choir	5
Football	4
Dance	4
Other sports	4
Gymnastics	3
Drama	3
Rugby	2
Rounders	2
ICT	2
Chess	1
Youth club	1
Guitar	1

These data suggest that Traveller students are willing to become involved in wider aspects of school life. Some children who did not take part were involved in clubs or activities run by other organisations. Seven of the boys went to boxing clubs, two girls had dancing classes and one girl was involved in majorettes. Travelling distance between home and school and reliance on school buses or parents' own transport sometimes restricted access to clubs but levels of participation were generally high. Of the 20 students who said they took no part in clubs or activities in Year 7, 13 left school during Key Stage 3, so this may be a factor associated with retention.

Involvement by parents

Opportunities for parental involvement generally tend to be more common in primary schools than secondary so it was unsurprising that more parents mentioned examples of their involvement during the Year 6 interviews than at any other time in the study. In the primary phase, it was not uncommon for Traveller parents to watch their children perform in plays and assemblies, concerts and sports days (17 parents mentioned this during their interviews). Hannah's mum had been a parent governor, Carly's mum worked in the attached playgroup and others said that they had accompanied school trips or helped with fund-raising activities. Once the children transferred to secondary school, only a couple of mothers said that they had been to concerts at the school, perhaps because secondary schools tend to stage fewer such events.

This is not to suggest that the parents in the study had no further contact with their children's teachers once they transferred. The vast majority of parental contact which did take place with secondary school however was related to individual issues or problems such as non-attendance or behavioural concerns (initiated by the school) or alleged bullying (initiated by the parents). These meetings tended to be on a one-to-one or small-scale level, usually involving the head of year.

Only one in three parents said they had been to parents' evenings in primary school and this proportion dropped further after secondary transfer. Three-quarters of the Traveller parents said they didn't go to secondary school parents' evenings. Some were quite open about their reasons why:

> It's not that I don't want to go, I'm embarrassed to go ... When you sit there, I don't know what to say to them, they're waiting for you to speak, but how can I talk to them about school when I never went to school because I didn't understand it? It's awkward and you feel embarrassed you know.

This extract reveals feelings of insecurity which were echoed by other mothers who said they wouldn't feel confident in that situation. The use of educational jargon put some mothers off: 'I didn't understand what they were saying about SATs' and others felt intimidated by the teachers' use of 'posh words' or were afraid that they would be made to feel 'ignorant'. Other responses revealed a fear of racist attitudes from people at school:

> That's something we don't really bother too much with. I mean maybe we should take the time but we don't because we feel out of place. Because when you do go down they look at you: 'what Gypsies?' And they all kind of stand back a little bit as if you're going to grab hold of them and hit them or something. It's silly. A lot of people have still got an attitude you know: 'Oh no Gypsies' and that's it.

This fear was reflected in other interviews with mothers who said they didn't attend parents' evenings because they were worried about 'mixing' and 'I don't like people gawping at me'. One mother said she would go, but only if there were other Traveller women there.

Other parents said they did not go because they had younger children at home (6), they were ill at the time (4), they had no way of getting there (4), they had other things on (3), they did not find them useful (2), or they forgot (2). It is also possible that some parents were unaware of these events if they relied on their children to read letters. One student withheld information about parents' evenings because teacher reports would be 'bad', and another told her mother that the parents' consultation day was a teacher training day instead.

Overall, these data suggest that although the majority of Traveller parents did not attend consultation evenings, this did not necessarily indicate a lack of interest or concern, although teachers did not always understand this.

> There was a parents evening after his second exclusion and she made an appointment to come but she never came. So I got the impression that the parents didn't particularly support the school (form tutor).

Traveller mothers showed interest in their children's education and usually provided a supportive response to schools whenever problems were flagged up. Equally, they had no hesitation in contacting the school if they had worries or concerns about their children. In four cases (Matthew, Bridget, Kizzy and Shane), parents had gone through the appeal process in order to gain much wanted places for their children. This type of contact is likely to be emotionally charged for parents and staff alike.

Aspirations and continuing education

At each stage of the research, participants' views about future engagement in education and vocational aspirations were collected and compared over time. Researchers asked the young people and their parents to predict what they would be doing (or would like to do) as young adults. Their responses over the three year period are presented in Appendix 1.

Shelley and Leanne held particular professional aspirations that were sustained over the three year period, which were supported by their mothers. Shelley had always dreamed of training as a midwife, whereas Leanne wanted to be dance teacher. Both girls said they planned to travel and work abroad before settling into their careers. Crystal and Kizzy both considered a range of graduate profession options and even had the backing of their mothers to go to university, if that was what they wanted.

Bridget changed her mind frequently and spoke of a variety of aspirations, including teaching, which was supported by her mother. In Year 9 her aspirations became lower. The same applied to Marie: she and her mother began to voice reservations about the cost of higher education when interviewed in Year 8. Gemma, Hannah and Helena on the other hand became more ambitious over the three year period. Although Hannah did not transfer to secondary school, and said in Year 6 that she would be helping her mum at home, she expressed a desire to study IT when she was interviewed at the age of 14. Eileen's aspirations appeared to fluctuate in line with those of her best friend.

Becky and Chelsea had not been expected by their mothers to complete Key Stage 3. Becky mentioned a few vocational preferences but did not show any great commitment as she thought she would be excluded from school. Chelsea seemed more determined and wanted to train as a hairdresser. Kimberly expected to go into factory work, like her sisters.

Danny and David were expected by their parents to follow and work with their male relatives but both these boys expressed a desire to move away from these pre-determined futures and make their own decisions. Shane was unsure about his future but did not see himself taking up his father's business. Kenny dreamed of a career in professional football and no expectations were voiced by either Kenny or his mother about a traditional Traveller occupation.

Joe, on the other hand, always said that he wanted to learn the motor trade from male relatives and then establish his own car dealing business. Charlie also expected to go into business with his brother after Year 11. Kieran planned to follow in his granddad's footsteps and learn the building trade. Dean had expected to be working with his dad at 14 but transferred to a special school and in Year 9 said he planned to stay on another year before joining the family trade.

Fifteen students correctly predicted at the age of 11 that they would be out of school by the age of 14. Their parents also correctly predicted this outcome. This implies that over a third of the students transferred to secondary school with the expectation that this would be a temporary arrangement. The pull of cultural expectations is clearly a significant factor. In many cases the predicted withdrawal from school was preceded by a breakdown in relationships (such as bullying, disciplinary action by the school or impaired home-school relationships). Becky and Chelsea were the only students who completed Key Stage 3 against their mothers' expectations but these mothers continued to express their worries about staying on at school.

Conflicting messages about the value of secondary education may well lead to cultural dissonance. As one secondary school teacher speculated:

> In a school you have the ethos of working for a reason, you want good qualifications etc. and then if they are listening to [other] girls who have dreams or plans and they know they can't have those dreams, then it must be difficult for them.

Another teacher pointed out, 'Our message is 'life is what you want to make of it' but I wonder to what extent they are in charge of their future.'

The study certainly found evidence of fixed attitudes and expectations which supported and promoted traditional adult roles for Traveller men and women. Of the 39 parents who were interviewed over the course of the study, over half (20) gave responses which indicated a wish or expectation for their children to follow traditional and cultural gender-based roles. For the boys this meant self-employment in a traditional Traveller occupation, often in conjunction with male relatives; for the girls the future centred around marriage, childcare and domestic duties.

> It's very important that she helps me at home, because the sort of life that she's going to marry into, which will be the Travelling life, she needs to be able to make a good home ... I'll start moulding her for the life that I want for her (Hannah's mother).

Converging views were expressed by their children. There were no cases where parents and children expressed opposing views on this matter.

> Next year I'll be at home learning how to clean up and do things like that, helping me mum ... we don't really get jobs and that or do GCSEs or anything. We usually stay at home until we're 18, 19 and then usually get married and then be a house-wife (Sarah-Jane).

Fifteen of the parents, however, gave responses that appeared to challenge or diverge from traditional attitudes and norms. This group was largely composed of the parents of the retained students. Again, the children of this group echoed their parents' expectations. One boy who lived on an unauthorised site proudly stated:

> I'm doing triple science so I'll get three GCSEs from that, I'm doing History, Classical Civilisation, because they link in with each other, and my two sub-options are business studies and RE.

Four of the parents changed their minds over the course of this study. That may indicate shifting attitudes, or it may have been that they felt under pressure to give what they thought was the 'right' response.

Conflicting concepts of 'adulthood' and 'childhood' present a prime example of cultural dissonance. The age at which childhood ends and adulthood begins is a fluid social and cultural construct. The raising of the school leaving age to sixteen and developments in education policy towards an increasingly academic curriculum may have widened the gap further. Recent moves towards a more flexible and vocational curriculum at Key Stage 4 may help to remedy this. On the other hand, this will come too late for students who leave the system before the end of Key Stage 3.

Points for reflection
* Could schools do more to recognise and value the skills and abilities which Traveller children are taught at home? Would it be possible to legitimise their vocational skills by incorporating them into work experience or alternative education packages? As Marie suggested, 'They should put a bit more in there for the

Travellers. Maybe landscaping or something, or farm work. Make them feel that there's something in there for them as well'.

- To what extent do secondary schools consult with Traveller students about the ways in which their culture is recognised and valued in school? Do schools, TES and parents sometimes 'impose' their well-intentioned ideas to raise awareness? This study found that young Travellers in secondary schools felt awkward about this and were more concerned with fair treatment. A consultative review of the 'hidden curriculum', including an audit of school policies and practices would be a good starting point.

- The formality of parents' evening may be too daunting for many Traveller parents. This may be interpreted by schools as showing a lack of interest or support. How can schools help to build trusting relationships with Traveller parents and avoid the scenario where contact is seen as socially threatening or is always related to a 'problem?'

- Do our visions of 'inclusive schooling' take full account of all the ways in which students can be disenfranchised? Do they recognise that some students may be negotiating competing cultural norms and values within a primarily ethnocentric school culture.

- Could participation in the informal curriculum of secondary schools be developed and encouraged as part of a strategy to improve retention of Gypsy Traveller students?

- Can too much focus on cultural explanations about retention encourage low expectations and divert attention away from the problem of racism?

Note
1   Romani word meaning rabbit (signifying timidness)

6

Racism:
encounters and responses

This chapter reports on the nature and prevalence of racism in school as perceived and described by the students in the study and their parents. It looks at the ways in which the young Travellers and their parents identified and dealt with experiences of racial bullying and how schools and teachers responded. Due to the sensitivity of the information in this section, pseudonyms have been used sparingly in order to ensure complete anonymity.

Bullying behaviour, including racial bullying can be physical, verbal or psychological (Olweus, 1993; Smith and Sharp, 1994). The key component of bullying is that physical or psychological intimidation is repeated over a period of time and produces a pattern of harassment and abuse (Batsche and Knoff, 1994). A large-scale study of Sheffield schools (Whitney and Smith, 1993) found that ten per cent of secondary age students were sometimes bullied. In a more recent study by Cline *et al* (2002) which investigated the experiences of ethnic minority students in mainly white schools, it was found that over a third of the children encountered racial name-calling or verbal abuse either at school, or during the school journey. In approximately half of these cases, the racial harassment had been endured for an extended period of time. The nature and prevalence of racism encountered by Traveller students in schools was first brought sharply into focus almost twenty years ago by the Swann Report

(DES, 1985) and by Acton and Kenrick (1985). According to Ofsted (1996) 'too many' Traveller students in secondary schools were probably excluded as a result of disruptive responses to racial abuse. More recently, a study of Travellers in Scottish secondary schools found that much of what the schools saw as indiscipline in the form of violence might have been in response to racist name-calling from other students (Lloyd *et al*, 1999). In the previous chapter, it was revealed that some Traveller students attempted to mask or disguise their ethnicity, (or 'play white' according to Cline *et al*), and it was suggested that this was one of a number of coping strategies some Travellers adopt to protect themselves from racial abuse and other forms of social exclusion which emanate from a predominantly hostile and prejudiced majority culture (Hancock, 1997).

Racism in the wider community

Generally, headteachers recognised that despite efforts to challenge and combat racism within their schools, prejudice amongst the wider community was a pervasive force.

> We don't have too much of a problem with the children. It is a bit more of an issue with the parents (primary school headteacher).

This view was typical of more than half of the primary school headteachers (17) who made reference to hostile attitudes and actions such as petitions against Travellers in the local community. Only one primary headteacher spoke of positive relationships in the local community. This was a rural area where the Traveller community had been established for a number of years and was valued for its contribution to the agricultural economy.

Negative attitudes and perceptions in the community sometimes affected relationships in school, where there was objection in principle to the school admitting Traveller students, as in three cases, or where parents saw the Traveller students as receiving special treatment or positive discrimination as in three other cases. Billy's primary headteacher reported that in the past parents had started to take their children away from the school as more Traveller students arrived. Similarly, when Louis and Seamus moved to a new primary school, there was initial 'uproar' from other parents but, as the headteacher explained: 'when they realised their own kids were making friends, no-one came back [to complain]'. Another headteacher described how shocked she had been to hear that one girl was not allowed to invite her Traveller friend to her birthday party.

As one interviewee put it: 'racism is endemic in the community' and another described how difficult it was to shift entrenched attitudes which reflected: 'the psyche of generations'. TES staff interviewed also echoed the view that Travellers were generally mistrusted and treated with disdain by the settled community in the areas where they worked; 'there is a lot of prejudice in the area, Travellers are a despised group'.

Interviews with staff in secondary schools revealed a similar outlook, although there were fewer references made to this issue: 'We need to give kids more credit. It's the adults who are the ones with the problems about prejudice'. Those who did feel able to comment all mentioned prejudice, hostility or a general lack of tolerance from the local community and one person recognised that Travellers in the area had 'a lot to put up with'.

A couple of the teachers suggested that it was the highly mobile groups of Travellers who aroused the most mistrust and hostility from local residents, although both Connor's and Chelsea's mothers described how neighbours had reacted negatively when their families moved in to housing accommodation. Connor's family moved away after a few months but Chelsea's mother described how the behaviour of the local community continued to make her feel unwelcome and harassed on a regular basis:

> Anything goes wrong in this village, it's down to my house and that's what I get. 'Oh it must be the Gyppos' and believe it or not, we get that from old people. In fact it was my housing officer last year who asked me if I wanted to make a formal complaint because no matter what I do, I keep myself to myself, I don't bother with anybody. On one occasion I rescued a dog I fetched a dog here at 10 o'clock at night and by 9 o'clock the next morning I had the council on me doorstep. If I move my caravan from one side of my garden to the other, which I'm entitled to do because it's slabbed, they phone up and report me to the council. When I put a fence up they phoned up the council and reported me ... So the housing officer actually asked me if I wanted to make a complaint.

Two other mothers, who lived in relatively affluent rural settings, said they felt the village people 'looked down' on them. This suggests that the effects of direct or indirect racism are likely to be an integral part of Traveller students' life experience and may help to explain parental fears about their children's safety in school.

Racist name-calling in school

Information about students' direct experiences of name-calling or racial bullying in school was gathered throughout the course of the study. However, these findings should be treated with caution, due to the sensitivity of the subject and the fact that some children were interviewed in the presence of their parents. The researchers were sensitive to signs of discomfort and therefore avoided probing for information. These factors may have influenced the students' responses and their willingness to talk about their experiences. An anonymous survey might have yielded more reliable data. It was found that:

- More than half of the students interviewed in Year 6 (24) said that they were called racist names in primary school.

- Of those who transferred to secondary, the majority (29 out of 38 students) admitted that they had encountered some form of racial abuse, particularly during their first year in secondary school. This supports other findings that revealed an increase in bullying around the age of 11-12 (Whitney and Smith, 1993). Interviews with secondary school staff also revealed evidence of fights or arguments involving Traveller students in the early days after transfer.

- Only four of the students in the sample said they had not been called names in either primary or secondary school. Of this group, the two boys had left before the end of Key Stage 3, whereas both the girls stayed on. One girl was open about her identity but the other hid her cultural heritage.

- Two boys said that name-calling stopped once they reached secondary school. Both these boys completed Key Stage 3, were popular with non-Travellers in school but had an established support network with other Travellers.

- Three-quarters (fifteen) of the students who completed Key Stage 3 said that they had been called names or bullied at some stage in secondary school. In most cases students said that it was an occasional rather than a regular occurrence, although, in a handful of cases, the abuse apparently took place over several weeks or had continued intermittently into Year 9. One girl claimed that she was bullied 'nearly every day ... when people don't call me [names] I love school to bits'.

In another case, a boy had told the researcher in Year 6:

> They don't know how much name-calling we get. I'd say it happens about twice a week to me. Sometimes I tell a teacher but sometimes I just take no notice. It's usually only a couple of kids. They call me 'Gypsy' in a nasty way.

In Year 7, the same boy was bullied 'almost immediately' and this went on unreported and undetected for several weeks. The student was threatened with a pair of scissors not to tell.

> I would put up with it for three days and then on the next couple of days things were better so I would just try to block it and think it had stopped now, but then, it got so bad in the end I told [name of sister].

The nature of verbal abuse

Students who spoke about their experiences of name-calling were asked what kind of things the other students said to them. Their responses included direct abuse using racist vocabulary: 'Gypsy', 'Smelly Gypsy', 'Smelly Gyppo', 'Smelly Pikey', as well as pejorative slurs on Traveller lifestyle and negative stereotypes: 'Farm girl', 'Nature boy', 'Tramp', 'Skiver', 'Thief'. Students' homes were called 'shopping trolleys', 'cardboard boxes' and 'dustbin wagons' and there was teasing about a perceived lack of washing facilities: 'they'll say things like, um 'go and wash in the river' and all this'. Two students said that people made derogatory rhymes from their names in a way that incorporated negative stereotypes. Five students said that their mothers were called whores or prostitutes.

As well as open and direct name-calling, there was also evidence of a more subtle form of verbal abuse: 'Every time I walked past they'd say 'Oooh let's do the River Dance!' Another student said:

We went on this trip to the Victorian museum and there were some bow-top wagons there, and this girl said 'I don't like him 'cos he's a Gypsy'. She said it so I would hear. I was really enjoying that trip 'til then. Then she spoilt it for me.

Physical abuse

Six students (four boys and two girls) reported physical attacks in secondary school. Of this group, four were still in school at the end of Year 9. The girls had been subjected to occasional bullying behaviour such as pushing, tripping up and having food thrown at them. One of the boys had items of his uniform and his school bag torn or stolen and his shoes were flushed down the toilet. Another boy had his nose broken, a third was pushed down some stairs and the fourth was threatened with scissors.

How students responded

Reporting

When the students were asked how they dealt with experiences of name-calling or bullying, their responses were mixed. Eleven of the students (38 per cent) who had encountered bullying or verbal abuse said they reported it to a teacher. Follow-up comments, however, implied that this was not the only strategy that they had used and the figure may therefore be unreliable. The findings from a nationwide study in Ireland (O'Moore, Kirkham and Smith, 1997) found that only sixteen per cent of secondary age students who were bullied chose to report it to teachers. Smith and Shu (2000) and Cline *et al* (*op cit*) also discovered that a lack of trust in official reporting procedures led to alternative strategies such as the reliance on older siblings for protection. In this study, interviews with parents and teachers generally confirmed what the students told the researchers, and there were very few cases where teachers were unaware that bullying or name-calling might have taken place. However, it may be that teachers' awareness was raised by acts of physical retaliation. Also, accounts from students suggested that reporting an incident was more likely for serious rather than routine instances, so it may be that the teachers were unaware of the whole picture. For example, Charlie said that he was 'not the sort of person to go telling a teacher every time'. On most occasions he preferred to settle it himself, only telling a teacher when things got 'out of hand'.

Reasons for not reporting included the belief that allegations would not be treated seriously by staff: 'Some teachers just say 'don't tell tales' when you report it'. Stephen, Bridget and Linda all intimated that the teachers would be less likely to believe Traveller students if the perpetrators denied the allegation. The underlying perception here was that institutional racism pervaded the system and prevented fair treatment: 'the other kids just deny it so we don't bother,' 'they said it was me and the teachers believed them'.

> If somebody called me a 'Gyppo' I would hit them. Right? I would hit them! Because that's racism ... but the teachers, they don't respect that. They think to themselves 'now as you're a Traveller, you've done it all'. I reckon that goes on (Linda).

Other students like Becky and Joe said that reporting led to further retaliation: 'you get called more names for being a grass' whereas Kieran spoke about losing face through reporting: 'You're called soft if you go to a teacher. If you go to a teacher, you're called a chicken'. This view was also taken by one of the form tutors, who explained it in terms of a cultural phenomenon:

> The major culture clash is ... we as a school say to the kids: 'You do not sort out your own problems. You don't fight, you let somebody else deal with it, and then you don't get into trouble'. And all the Traveller children I know have an attitude that if you are not seen to be sorting out your own problems you are weak. You have failed. And it is not just the boys, the girls are exactly the same. It is a culture thing, that allowing somebody else to sort out your problems is seen as a sign of weakness. And almost all the problems we have are how do you get them to understand that us arbitrating and using the systems isn't a sign of weakness, it is a sign of strength?

Physical retaliation

Other evidence from interviews with students and their parents supported this teacher's theory of a parental and cultural expectation which conflicted with school policy. One mother told the researcher: 'I've told them to stand up for themselves. But the teachers are telling them not to hit back'. Another revealed a similar expectation when talking about her fears of bullying:

> There's quite a lot of people round here that's took the children out because they just can't cope with the stress and the

> children being beat up all the time. You see we kind of like keep pushing our children saying 'you hit back' but obviously you can't if they're 17 and 18 year-old – it goes up to 18 year-old you see and he's not 13 until March.

This may represent another example of cultural dissonance. Although the students were apparently aware of the reporting procedures that their schools promoted, at least a third of the students (fifteen) had retaliated physically in primary school. A slightly larger proportion (two-fifths) of those who transferred to secondary school had been reprimanded at least once for physical acts which were responses to name-calling or bullying behaviour. More than half of these Traveller students were girls, although it may be that altercations between boys did not always come to the attention of teachers. While cultural influences pertaining to a long history of persecution may have some part to play in determining students' responses: 'My people say if someone hits you, you must hit back', the reluctance for students to report incidents suggests that a combination of factors may lead to students dealing with bullies in alternative ways, including physical aggression.

In some cases students had developed or earned a reputation for being 'hard' and this could offer some protection from racial abuse and bullying (Connolly, 1998). Teachers were also able to identify these traits: 'She is a lovely girl but she has a side to her that you don't want to mess with!' Several of the boys were involved in boxing clubs and were physically strong. Kieran, Joe, Becky and Kimberley all felt that their reputations made others more wary about picking on them: 'They know I'll stick up for meself.'

Peer support

In a few other cases, students were known to have the support of older Travellers and, as some teachers suggested, this could act as a deterrent to potential bullies. 'They've only got to tip the wink at home and there's a posse waiting!' (head of year).

> I don't think Louis was beyond threatening the Travelling community on the other pupils. You know,' take me on and you take the whole lot of us on' (head of year).

Joe told the researcher that children should sort bullies out themselves. When asked: 'What about kids who can't sort it out for themselves?' he replied:

> Well that's why kids like that get in with people like me and that. They'll come and tell us and we'll say: 'Oi leave him alone, you're bigger than 'im, you know your stronger than he is so just leave him alone. There's no need for it'. So they leave them alone because they don't wanna start arguments with us. There's a big gang of us. We don't hang around with one another at school but we know if anyone gets in bother then words gets around and we know we'll all be there for one another. I know at least fifty people what I know will stick up for me. I know loads of people in each year [group]. Nobody will pick on [younger brother] when he comes up!

Other students, such as Helena and Kieran mentioned non-Traveller friends who had defended them and challenged racial comments made by others. This was also mentioned by a TES teacher working in a different school who had observed that: 'although there are racist incidents in school – there are a lot of kids who will rebuke and say 'Hey! You can't say that ... that's out of order!'"

Avoidance

There was also some evidence to suggest that avoidance strategies were sometimes adopted by students who were being bullied. For example, Linda's attendance level in primary school suddenly dropped around the time when she later admitted she had been bullied. Louis was said to react by running away from school and David and Becky both pretended to be ill during known periods of bullying. Marie, on the other hand resisted the temptation to avoid bullies in her school:

> Researcher: Did you ever feel during that time that you didn't want to go to school?
>
> Marie: Sometimes. But like, if you don't go, they'll just think 'Oh look, I'm tough! Because she's staying away from school! She must be scared!' So you don't give them that satisfaction.

Other strategies such as making friends with the bullies (6), responding with verbal rebukes (5), and ignoring taunts (3) were identified from the interview transcripts. Some students said they would deal with bullying in their own way but did not specify how. One girl started smoking in Year 6 in an attempt to cope with the stress of bullying and later, in Year 8, had difficulties in sleeping, according to her mother, who said she had been 'pacing up and down the floor ... worried what's going to happen the next day'.

Parental and sibling involvement

Where students' disclosed experiences of bullying or name-calling to their parents or older siblings, this usually resulted in swift action being taken by mothers, who went to the school to speak to a senior member of staff. In Kimberley's case, her mother contacted the other girls' parents directly. In a few cases, TES teachers were asked by parents to act as mediators by helping arrange a meeting or act as an advocate for them.

Inter-racial tension

Ten of the students attended secondary schools with culturally diverse populations. Of these, four students, all boys, made reference to inter-racial tension between groups of Traveller and Asian students. There was a perception amongst this group that Asian students were the 'aggressors' and that the teachers took racist allegations more seriously if they were waged against black and Asian students rather than Travellers. Inter-racial conflict was also recognised by the TES staff in those areas. One teacher described the situation as a 'them and us' culture in which neither community showed respect or tolerance for the other.

School responses

Where senior school staff had been alerted to name-calling or bullying by the parents of the victims, this was usually seen to be dealt with effectively at the time by the mothers and students concerned. However, some students felt that their own reporting was not taken seriously enough. TES staff had mixed opinions but generally felt that the effectiveness of the response was largely dependent on the head of year concerned: 'The school is intellectually, very aware of the race dimension but practically, it depends on the head of year's response'. This view was echoed by some of the headteachers who said that heads of year were relied upon to use their best judgement and take appropriate action.

A key problem appeared to be that systems of support and official procedures to address and deal with race-related bullying relied upon children and parents reporting them (also noted by Cline *et al*, 2002). In three cases, signs of bullying were initially identified by TES staff working in schools, who then alerted teachers and parents. A good deal of the racial abuse was likely to go unreported and if the bullying behaviour took place outside the classroom, during breaks, moving between lessons and on the journey to and from school, it was even more likely to be undetected (Kelly and Cohen, 1988; Jordan, 2001). Furthermore, a number of students maintained that unless a member of staff had actually overheard or witnessed an act of racial harassment, then they were unwilling to take action.

> It just annoys me when Miss don't hear them and don't do nowt about it. I tell the teachers. I say 'Miss he's just called me' and they say 'well I didn't hear it'. They say if they don't hear it they can't do nothing about it.

A few of the teachers admitted that it was difficult to distinguish between genuine allegations and 'hearsay' and there was an underlying suspicion in some cases, that the Traveller student concerned may well have incited the action by calling names first. The following extract reveals a less than sympathetic response from one head of year:

> They don't like the word 'Gypsy' ... or 'Gyppo' or whatever, and on occasions we have dealt with pupils who have said that to them but equally, they can come back with some of their technical language.

Another head of year admitted that it was difficult to confront racist attitudes without making them more entrenched: 'because what you can do is make a huge thing about it and they may focus on it more than they were focusing on it before! You know, people say things, not because it's the focus of their life or anything, they just say it!' The approach here was to support the victim rather than challenge the perpetrator.

During the final round of interviews in 2003 senior staff in schools were asked about the impact of the Race Relations (Amendment) Act (2000) on their policies and practice in school and, in particular, how this might affect Traveller students. Although most schools were able to provide Race Equality policy documents, this area of questioning revealed a fairly limited awareness amongst heads of year who were interviewed. Six felt unable to respond or comment. Other respondents implied that the RRAA would have no or little impact because their schools already put into practice all that was required of them (5), there were so few ethnic minority students on roll (3), or there was a perception of 'no problem here' (3).

> We have obviously had to look at the new Act in relation to the school policies but the school policies seem to meet the Act in every way anyhow. And ... the kids who could be subject to racial taunts, abuse, are anyway, really are just seen as regular kids and there hasn't been a problem.

In three schools the heads of year were sure that student data were monitored by ethnicity but others, with small numbers of Travellers, said that this was difficult or not applicable. However one of the schools which carried out ethnic monitoring had failed to include Travellers in a recent race equality survey.

The logging of racial incidents was mentioned by seven heads of year. In two cases there was no distinction between racial harassment and other kinds of bullying. When asked for clarification as to whether racist name-calling would be treated as racial harassment or bullying, one head of year replied: 'Bullying. I would class it more as bullying'. This perception is at odds with the distinction made in the Swann Report (DES, 1985). Most TES teachers said that they had not been involved in any training to do with the implementation of the RRAA in the schools. One TES teacher observed:

> I think policies about inclusion and monitoring performance of ethnic minorities and all that needs to be rigorously checked. And I think training programmes need to be built into the schools as a must. There's a whole lot needs doing.

Perceived racist attitudes of school staff

Some students and parents told the researchers they felt that certain teachers exhibited negative, racist or biased attitudes in relation to Travellers. This would support similar findings by Kenny (1997) and Clay (1999) in their studies of Traveller students in school. TES staff also picked up negative feelings or even open hostility in a couple of cases. One TES teacher described how a member of the school administration team had made disparaging remarks about the display of Traveller resources in a public area. Others made the following observations:

> Frankly, they don't want Travellers there. It's an uphill struggle! ... It's not a supportive environment, it's not a friendly environment, it's not a welcoming environment. I don't think they feel valued as a culture, valued as a group. They very quickly feel 'they don't want us'.

> One of the teachers ... she really disliked Travellers and she told me that on the first day! She is not representative of the whole staff but she is quite free with her comments.

> You're fighting prejudice. They talk about 'them'. It's hard work.

When asked whether they ever got into trouble at school, thirteen of the students in Year 6 added that they felt they were sometimes treated unfairly by teachers or lunchtime staff. They perceived that they were picked on or were given harsher treatment than non-Traveller students. A similar number of students (14) sensed that certain teachers in the secondary school held negative attitudes towards them (although only six of these were the same students who said the same thing in primary school). The extracts below illustrate the kinds of perceptions these students held:

> They don't pick on the other children. They know we're Travellers so they pick on us and not them. That's not fair.

> He ignores me and treats me different to everyone else.

> I think sometimes the teachers see me as the 'bad' person.

> He didn't like me from the start and I didn't like him. If I get put in his set next year I'm gonna give him hell. I'm sure he's got a thing about Travellers.

> They say 'Oh we treat everyone as equals' but I've never found that. Teachers never treat Travellers as equals because we're not good enough for them.

According to the accounts given by some senior managers in schools, these feelings may not be entirely without foundation. One head of year admitted that, as a staff 'we are still very negative in how we see them, to be honest'. Another senior teacher gave the following full and frank response:

The majority of the staff welcomed them with open arms, tried very hard with them. But I have to say, and I am ashamed to say it ... a very small minority were terrible. They had had bad experiences with Travellers in the past and allowed that to cloud their judgement and were not prepared to give [the Traveller pupils] a chance at all. As far as they were concerned, they were thieves from the minute they walked into the building, they were vagabonds and they never gave them a chance, no matter how many times I took these staff to one side and said ' you can't'. They were totally unprofessional in their approach ... there were certainly times when I witnessed them on a corridor perhaps disciplining them for something they wouldn't discipline another child for because of who they were. So that did create difficulties. I'm ashamed to say that but I have got to tell the truth.

Experiences of racism could make students guarded and sensitive, even with teachers they generally got on with, as this head of year discovered:

He was messing about and giving it this and I said 'Don't you go giving me any jip' and he said 'What did you call me?' I said 'J-I-P as in being cheeky not ...' You know, I didn't think twice about it but it's obviously something they are very sensitive about so I was able to set that straight. It makes me realise how aware of it they are even though it doesn't seem to be an issue.

Points for reflection

Direct quotations from the students in the study are used here to promote reflection and discussion about ways forward:

> There is one dinner lady who is really nice and kind to me. She is my favourite person here. If I get called names I go and see her – not the teachers. And I wouldn't tell the head. He wouldn't take it seriously.

• How many other students have a trusted adult to turn to in school? Is the trusted adult adequately trained and prepared to support the student effectively? How do teachers convince students that their allegations will be taken seriously?

> The teachers say 'I'll tell them off later' but they don't. I reckon they should follow it up and maybe make them stay in for a few playtimes because it mostly happens when we are outside.

- Do victims always receive feedback to reassure them that matters have been dealt with? What measures could be taken to ensure that children feel safer in less structured and supervised situations such as lunch and break times and during movement around the school?

> I got off to a bit of a rough start because there were people from all different schools. They weren't too keen on the idea of Travellers 'cos they weren't used to having Travellers in their school.

- What more could be done to protect Traveller students from racist bullying during the period of transition to secondary school? What more could be done to heighten awareness in all schools?

> I do like coming to school, it's just that it gets me down sometimes and I just take days off. The people get me down. Picking on me.

- How can schools ensure that vulnerable pupils are monitored effectively? Are absences analysed and picked up as a potential indicator of unhappiness?

> There's not a lot of bullying going on. The headteacher won't allow it. You get expelled.

- To what extent do other schools set high expectations and a culture of 'zero tolerance' which makes students feel safe?

> The teachers don't do anything 'cos I haven't really been to them when I get called names.

• Do teachers understand why students are reluctant to report racist name-calling and bullying? What can schools do to encourage a culture of reporting? How can schools break the silence and convince students that it is safe and effective to report bullying of themselves and others?

> Kids sort it out themselves and sometimes they get excluded if it leads to a fight. I don't think the teachers really get to the bottom of it sometimes.

• Are Traveller students being disproportionately excluded from school for fighting and aggression? How much of this behaviour is in response to racial harassment?

> I used to tell the teachers but they don't do nothing. They say that they'll put them in the racism book or something. But that's not a lot is it? Putting their name in a book!

• Are teachers and students clear about the purpose of logging racial incidents? How is the information then used to address and reduce levels of racism?

7

Slipping through the net?

This chapter focuses on those students from the sample who were no longer in the school system in Year 9 (academic year 2002-2003). It explores the reasons students were not retained in secondary school and presents some case studies to illustrate the events and circumstances that led to withdrawal from school. Particular factors, such as a breakdown in relationships with schools and cultural factors, which may influence the retention of Traveller students, are also identified. Other variables which may influence drop-out such as siblings' experience of secondary school, mobility, and school size are also considered. It concludes by presenting some points for reflection on the likelihood of certain students dropping out of school.

More than half the sample (24 students) were no longer in the school system in Year 9. Twice as many boys (16) had dropped out as girls (8). Despite the fact that that the original sample had slightly more boys (24) than girls (20), the gender difference in drop-out is notable.

When did students drop out?

Six students did not transfer to secondary school, which meant that:

- thirty-eight students from the sample attended during Year 7 (six dropped out during the year: two left at Christmas, one at Easter, two in the summer term and one at the end of Year 7).

- thirty-two attended in Year 8 (nine dropped out during the year: two left in the autumn, four in the spring, two in the summer and one at the end of Year 8).

- twenty-three went into Year 9 but three dropped out during the year (one at Christmas and two in the spring).

Case Studies

Four case studies illustrate the events and circumstances which meant that Ronnie, Linda, Carly and Peter were no longer in the school system in Year 9.

An examination of factors that might be associated with withdrawal from secondary school

Each of the case studies provide a list of possible factors that might be associated with students' withdrawal from secondary school. These and related factors are now explored to determine whether any patterns emerged across the cohort of 24 students who didn't stay at school.

Cultural influences and expectations

Cultural influences and expectations may impact on Traveller students' engagement in secondary school. The point of transfer to secondary school is a time when many young people within the Travelling communities are increasingly expected to take on more adult roles and responsibilities within their communities. It is also a time when some parents may want to remove their children from the perceived racist and negative influences of a '*gauje*' education and immerse them in a 'Traveller' education (Clay, 1999; Kiddle, 1999). Cultural influences and expectations were a factor in the withdrawal of most of the 24 students in the sample who were not engaged in education in Year 9, although the strength of such influences was variable. Parental interviews from the students who didn't stay at school revealed that the majority made statements which emphasised the benefits of a Traveller education:

> They're getting their own education from their brothers and their fathers learning how to fix motors and learning how to get their living. They are learning an education at home (Glyn's mother).

Case study 1 Ronnie

Ronnie was the eldest of five children and lived on a local authority site. His parents did not attend school and were not literate. He attended his final primary school for two years. At this school Traveller students accounted for 17 per cent of the school roll. Ronnie was open about his identity but tended to mix only with Traveller students at both primary and secondary school.

Ronnie's literacy and numeracy skills were very poor; he achieved a Level 1 (teacher assessment) in his Key Stage 2 SATs. He was not on the Code of Practice despite his poor basic skills. His mum felt that he did not receive enough support for his learning needs at primary school. There was 0.4 of a TES teacher supporting 52 Traveller students in Ronnie's primary school and he received literacy support from the TES twice a week but he often missed this because he arrived late at school. The TES also provided transition support to all Traveller students in Year 6. Ronnie transferred with four other Traveller students from his primary school. At secondary school, there was limited TES support for Traveller students for the first half-term of Year 7 but after that, due to staffing difficulties, there was no TES support, which resulted in all the Traveller students at the secondary school dropping out. When a new TES teacher was appointed she integrated them back into school with varying degrees of success. Both TES and school staff felt that Ronnie's progress was hindered by his poor attendance and at primary school he had often arrived late. His attendance at secondary school was very poor: in Year 7 it was 24 per cent and in Year 8 he only attended two sessions.

Ronnie's parents did not support secondary education: there was a belief that he should be out earning his living at 13. His mum also expressed concerns about drugs, smoking and sex education at secondary school, that he would be picked on because he could not read or write and because he was a Traveller. There was little contact between home and his primary school and virtually no contact with the secondary school. Ronnie felt isolated in secondary school as he was not in the same classes as his Traveller friends. He was also overwhelmed by the size of the school and wanted to return to his primary school. He could not access the curriculum.

Possible factors:

– Cultural factors: both Ronnie and his mum said that he would be out working by the time he was 13.

– Lack of support for his learning needs at both primary and secondary school: he was not on the Code of Practice, which meant that he was unable to access the curriculum. His TES teacher felt that he did not cope at all in Year 7 and regretted that the service was unable to provide him with additional support.

– History of poor attendance at primary school: this meant that he was unlikely to attend secondary school. Ronnie felt there was little point in attending because he could not access the curriculum.

Case study 2 Linda

Linda was the eldest of six children. Her family lived on unofficial roadside sites and tended to move within and between three counties. The family was moved on every couple of weeks. Little was known of her educational history: there appeared to be little, if any, passing on of educational records. Linda had attended her Year 6 primary school when she was younger and her family were living in the area. She returned to this school in Year 6. The school had a number of housed Travellers on roll. Her learning difficulties were felt by her teachers to be due to the disruption in her education. She was not entered for Key Stage 2 SATs, but had a reading ability of between eight and nine years.

Linda's parents applied to a secondary school which was not the usual transfer route for students from her primary, although family friends were attending this school. Linda attended the induction day and liked it but the family moved to a different county over the summer. In January of Year 7 she attended a secondary school for three weeks but did not like it and then the family moved. She attended another couple of schools briefly between Year 7 and Year 9 but the family's highly mobile lifestyle meant that her attendance was very limited and Linda was becoming more and more resistant to school.

Linda's Mum was very unsure about secondary transfer. She made the 'right noises' to the TES but she needed Linda at home. Linda recognised her family responsibilities: there needed to be someone in the trailer at all times and help was needed with her autistic brother.

The TES had a liaison-only role in her Year 6 primary school but had provided learning support when she was younger. Focused transition work in Year 6 might have been beneficial but the family's mobility meant that they had moved on by the time she was due to transfer. The TES provided a great deal of support in secondary school for Linda when she was in and for the family especially in relation to transport. The family relied on the TES and LEA for transport, as Linda's mum had lost her licence. The TES provided in-school support for a part-time timetable negotiated for Linda in Year 9. She attended for one and a half days a week with some integration into classes with one-to-one support. This arrangement lasted for a few weeks until the family moved out of the area. Linda was not in a school long enough to settle.

Possible factors:

- Mobility: Linda's highly mobile lifestyle severely affected her attendance
- Lack of official support for the family – apart from that provided by TES
- Cultural factors: cultural/family expectations and responsibilities meant that it was difficult for her to access a secondary education

Case study 3 Carly

Carly was the middle child of seven children living on a local authority site. She attended primary school from reception and her attendance was good when she was on the site. The family travelled but her mum put them in school wherever they were stopping. She was described as 'very quiet and shy' but her confidence had increased towards the end of primary school. Her level of attainment was low and she was on Stage 2 of the Code of Practice. She was not entered for Key Stage 2 SATs but was given a teacher assessment of Level 2. At primary school, she received one-to-one support from the TES for two hours a week and in-class support in literacy and numeracy. At secondary school, she received support from the TES, in-class support from the school and used the integrated learning ICT package, 'Successmaker', to boost her basic skills. Carly said her mum and dad did not want her to go to secondary school and she thought she would be at home when she was 14. She did not want to go on the induction visit, she was 'scared and crying'. She was extremely reliant on other Traveller students whom she transferred to secondary school and was upset when her Traveller friend was moved to a higher ability group. She was not particularly socialised into school and did not settle at secondary school.

She transferred late because the family were travelling at the beginning of the autumn term. Her overall attendance in Year 7 was 44 per cent. By the end of November Year 8 she had only attended seven full days (overall attendance 14 per cent). Carly and her younger brother became school refusers. Her parents, the school, the EWS and the TES tried to encourage attendance by using a range of strategies including incentives and threats. Both school and her parents said that she was alright once she was in school; it was just 'getting her in'. Her TES teacher observed that she had difficulties accessing lessons and poor standards of behaviour from other pupils in lessons exacerbated this. A part-time timetable was negotiated but this was unsuccessful. The children's non-attendance caused a great deal of friction between their parents and Carly was very difficult with her mum. Her mum did not know why she did not want to go but said that a number of the Traveller children did not want to attend the school. The school felt that Carly's parents had done all they could in trying to get her to attend. The family moved away in February 2002 and Carly did not attend school in the new area.

Possible factors:

- School refuser: then her family moved away, which meant that there was no follow-up on attendance
- The lack of support of other Traveller students in secondary school: when she was unable to rely on them she experienced difficulties
- Attainment: low levels of attainment and difficulties accessing the curriculum
- The school environment: which was viewed as hostile and threatening
- Possible cultural factors: her parents were less supportive of secondary education than of primary
- Sibling influence: her older brother was also a school refuser and left in Year 9. Her older sister attended longer but also left early.

Case study 4 Matthew

Matthew was the second youngest of four children. His family lived in trailers on a farm and owned the land and farm buildings. His primary school had limited experience of Traveller students: Matthew and his sister were the first they were aware of. Matthew's levels of attainment were: Key Stage 2 SATs Level 3 in English and maths and Level 4 in science. His attendance was: Year 6: 88 per cent; Year 7 first term 97 per cent but for the whole of Year 7 it was 69 per cent; Year 8 38 per cent; Year 9 he was recorded as Travelling. He only attended for two days in Year 9. At primary school Matthew was on Stage 2 of the Code of Practice for learning and behaviour. At secondary school he was on 'School Action' for behaviour. At primary school he received some support from the TES: in Year 6 he had in-class support with some withdrawal for pastoral support. At secondary school, the TES provided pastoral support. In Year 6, Matthew's mum informed the TES that his class teacher had said to him that he would be better off at home 'because of his culture'. Matthew was becoming economically independent and was involved with his mum's horse breeding and livery business and his mum felt that the primary school found this difficult to cope with.

Matthew's behaviour deteriorated in Year 8 which was linked to family problems. He was excluded four times in Year 8, for three, two and two 15-day exclusions for defiance, assaults on students and staff, and verbal abuse. Matthew believed that he should fight back and his mum felt that Matthew was reacting to other students' behaviour but that these students were not excluded. He was educated in the Learning Support Unit (LSU) for most of Year 8 and the school felt that he made little academic progress: they were just trying to contain him. His TES teacher felt that he spent too much time in the LSU. Permanent exclusion was threatened at the end of Year 8 but mum sent Matthew to Ireland because of problems at home. In the autumn term of Year 9, he had a period of dual registration and attended the PRU. When he was reintegrated back into school in December, a violent confrontation with another student in the LSU led to his permanent exclusion on the day he was reintegrated.

Matthew's mum was supportive of school but did not feel that their way of life was understood or valued. She felt that the school did not know how to handle Matthew's behaviour. Both Matthew and his mum wanted him to be in school. His two older siblings attended the same secondary school but both had left early and his mum felt that Matthew would be identified with his older brother who was known as a 'fighter'.

Possible factors:

– Behavioural issues: Matthew's behaviour, particularly issues around his anger, was not fully addressed. The behaviour management strategies in school didn't meet his needs. The TES felt that he needed support and counselling to address his difficulties at home. Cultural norms and a belief that you should 'hit back' resulted in Matthew's exclusion for retaliating to bullying, which both he and his mum felt was unfair.

– Low expectations: the school's low expectations of his behaviour, attainment and attendance appears to be self-fulfilling prophecy.

Parents also saw participation within the Traveller economy as a way of maintaining cultural identities and boundaries. By the time they reached secondary age a couple of the students in the study were already relatively successful entrepreneurs who were involved in horse breeding and training. The 'pull' of economic independence was greater than the incentive to stay in school, as Christopher's uncle observed: 'He broke three horses in last summer for different people. It's all there; he's got his skills. Christopher when he's at school he's losing money'. The skills he had learnt were clearly perceived to lie outside the context of school. Not only did his work reap financial benefits, it also kept him away from the negative influences of the inner city neighbourhood in which he lived, including school. Work provided a positive alternative: 'It's better for him. Round here there's loads of drugs, there are drugs in the school ... the phone box at the end of the street, they're dealing from it' (Christopher's uncle).

Similarly, cultural influences and expectations influenced Traveller girls' staying on. For Hannah this was *the* reason she did not transfer to secondary school. For others, such as Sarah-Jane, it was the reason why she dropped out in Year 8: 'They'd [parents] rather me stop at 13 or 14 than go 'til 16 because we don't believe in people going until that age'. From Year 6 both Sarah-Jane and her mother said that she would stop attending when she was 13. For young people like Linda, living on the roadside with five younger siblings, including an autistic brother, family responsibilities were paramount.

Linked to cultural expectations and influences was a belief amongst parents whose children were no longer in school by the end of Key Stage 3, that they had learnt all they needed to know for their lifestyle; the rest of the *gauje* education was seen as irrelevant: 'If he had to go to school 'til he were 16 or 17 it wouldn't make no difference to him cos there'd be nowt that he could learn off of schooling' (Christopher's mother). The perceived irrelevance of the secondary curriculum is an issue for many disengaged students:

> It's a problem with white working class boys and it's becoming a problem with Bangladeshi boys too. We aren't able to offer something that seems to make sense to them (head of year).

However, many Traveller students had an alternative in terms of their participation in the Traveller economy.

If parents were satisfied that adequate literacy levels had been achieved, students might also stop attending: 'it might be a reading age of eight if that's the best in the family' (TES teacher). Parents saw the benefits of functional literacy: 'there's nothing else I want him to learn because he can read and write' (Nick's mother) but not necessarily the relevance of going beyond this level. Traveller students' self-determination as to whether they accessed school was also perceived as problematic: 'His mum asks him whether he wants to go to school, she doesn't say, 'go to school.' Every day it is a choice for him, and obviously if he is given a choice he is going to say 'no'" (TES teacher). This philosophy may reflect the parents' wisdom in not forcing their children into an unhappy and possibly racially abusive environment. TES staff also recognised the perceived irrelevance of secondary education for many Traveller families: 'I still feel I'm trying to sell them something they don't want to buy and 'Education Otherwise' is what a lot of Travellers want'.

Education Otherwise can be seen as a way in which Traveller students can 'slip through the net'. It is a mechanism by which parents can avoid prosecution but still not send their children to secondary school and, conversely, it is a way that the LEA and *gauje* society can deal with Traveller students' non-attendance at secondary school. A number of parents in the sample whose children dropped out of secondary education exercised their right to access 'Education Otherwise', i.e. educating their children at home. Concerns were expressed by TES staff about the lack of monitoring of such provision and described as a form of 'official truancy'. There were instances in this sample where parents threatened with prosecution elected for Education Otherwise, which meant that the school took the student off roll and there was little or no follow-up by the LEA. Seven parents applied for Education Otherwise over the course of the study but only one student was actually receiving any tuition in Year 9. The rise in the uptake of Education Otherwise, and monitoring such provision, was a growing issue in some LEAs:

> According to [the LEA] we have only got about six or eight children [applying for Education Otherwise] because the others

haven't filled their forms in. I have got a list of nearly 20 but because they haven't filled the forms in they don't count them as official figures (TES teacher).

Siblings' experience at secondary school

Apart from one, all the siblings of the students who didn't stay in secondary school also left secondary school early. Although over a third (nine) of the 24 students who dropped out did not have older siblings, which meant that there was no recent experience of secondary education in the immediate family, and three had older siblings who had not transferred to secondary school. Eight of the students who didn't stay on at school had siblings who had had negative experiences in secondary school including behavioural difficulties, exclusions, and attendance problems. In two instances TES staff and parents felt that the reputation of older siblings had influenced the secondary school's opinion of the Traveller students in the sample. Thus, older siblings' negative experiences of secondary school – generally to do with the attitudes of students, parents and school staff – might well have influenced the expectations and experiences of younger siblings who left school.

Accommodation and mobility

Of the group of students who left during Key Stage 3:

• fourteen lived on local authority sites

• five were housed

• four lived on private sites

• one was on the roadside.

When these figures were compared with the original sample, they showed that the proportion of students who lived on local authority sites were slightly over-represented in the numbers of students who dropped out of secondary school.

Was mobility a factor in students' withdrawal from school? The only highly mobile student in the sample was Linda, and her mobility did affect her ability to access school. However, there were also links between mobility and non-attendance for other students in the sample. For nearly two-thirds (15) of the students who left school, mobility, whilst not directly linked to their withdrawal, may have been a factor in reinforcing their non-attendance once they had dropped out of school. For example, Carly, Clint, Stephen and Sarah-Jane stopped attending and then their families moved away, which made following up their attendance extremely difficult, as a parent observed: 'They [the LEA] don't know she's there, she don't go to school. I just tell them she's back with my mum'. Similarly, Nick's attendance at secondary school was very poor: 'A few women came down over him not being in school, but then we shifted [at the end of Year 7]'. By the time they returned in Year 8 'he hadn't been in for so long so they don't bother' (Nick's mother). In such situations mobility was perhaps used as an avoidance strategy. TES staff were also well aware that if too much pressure was put on families they could 'just up and move' (TES teacher).

Attainment and curriculum access

Low attainment and difficulties accessing the curriculum may have impacted on the withdrawal of a quarter (6) of those students who dropped out. A full breakdown of students' SATs results are provided in Appendix 2. The number of students in the sample operating below Level 3, particularly in English, gives cause for concern. Nearly a third (14) of the sample were operating below Level 3 in English and maths which would impact on their ability to access the curriculum with confidence at secondary school. Three students who achieved Level 4 in science had difficulties with literacy, which meant that they had to rely on amanuensis. These were difficulties they were going to encounter at the secondary level.

Although Seamus was statemented and well supported at primary school, both TES and primary school staff felt that his learning needs and age – he was two years older than his peers – meant that he would experience difficulties at secondary school. Similarly, Ronnie, Stephen and Ben's inability to access the curriculum, as well as their poor attendance, was seen as having a negative effect on their staying on at secondary school. In addition, a lack of support for students' learning needs was identified as a factor that may have influenced Ben, Ronnie, Stephen and Christopher to drop out of school. Ronnie observed when interviewed in Year 8: 'I can't do the work it's too hard – I can't read nor write'. In Year 7, despite having a reading age that was six years below his chronological age, Ronnie was not on the Code of Practice and only received limited additional support from the TES:

> Ronnie never coped in Year 7 and I really regret that we weren't able to give him more support ... he was being set up to fail because how could he access a secondary curriculum when his skills were so poor without support? (TES teacher).

Schools' low expectations of Traveller students' attainment were also seen as having a detrimental impact on their retention:

> I have been in meetings ... where the [member of school staff] has said 'we can't have him in this school, we don't want him in this school' ... Instead of saying 'we actually want you to work and we want you to do well', it is attitude really (TES teacher).

Attendance and engagement

Attendance was clearly an issue for a number of Traveller students who dropped out. Nearly three-fifths (14) of those who dropped out had attendance issues, which may have influenced their non-retention, and a quarter (six) of them started primary school late. Ronnie and Nick's poor levels of attendance at primary school continued and deteriorated in secondary school. Their poor attendance at secondary school meant that they were never there long enough to be integrated into school:

> He [Nick] has never had an opportunity to settle in. He doesn't know where he is supposed to be on his timetable if he does go in ... So he is sort of I expect like an outsider, practically all the time that he is there (TES teacher).

These comments also indicate the alienation of poor attenders in secondary school; these students had nothing to keep them in school. This sense of alienation was further reinforced by the reactions of staff and students when they were in school: 'When they miss and come back they do create us problems' (head of year). The TES teacher echoed this view: 'I doubt he was made very welcome when he was there'.

Similarly, Matthew's mother felt that the school expected him to drop out, like his older siblings had done. She said that a member of staff had said to her:

'[Name of sister] went when she were 14, [name of brother] went when he were nearly 15. How old's Matthew going to be when he goes?' So they're expecting him to go. [He said] 'When young boys like Matthew get to 13-year old they never come back to school they just disappear into the community and we never see them again'. And he more or less said 'just take him and go'.

Other pressures within secondary schools meant that in some instances Traveller students' non-attendance was not followed up as quickly or as thoroughly as it might have been: 'The workload and the attendance problems we have in school, are such that severe cases like that are on the back burner' (head of year). There was also confusion about the monitoring of Traveller students' attendance, which resulted in Connor dropping out of school without the TES being informed. This perhaps supports the argument that schools should be taking responsibility for monitoring Traveller students' attendance. Connor, Ben and Billy's attendance at secondary school was initially satisfactory but then dropped off quite dramatically, reflecting a need to explore the reasons for this. Connor's school was not aware of the reasons for his absence, whilst Peter's non-attendance was perhaps not followed up as thoroughly as it might have been because his family lived in one county and he attended school in another:

So nobody is going to chase them up. Obviously we've told people they're not in school but nobody chases it up. It's a [name of county] school but it would be [name of different county] Education Welfare Service but as he's off roll he's just lost to the system (TES teacher).

The above comments also draw attention to the issue of schools taking Traveller students off roll without following up what happens to them. Nevertheless, the attendance of a quarter (six) of the students who dropped out was good up to the time they withdrew from school, so clearly for these students attendance was not a factor in their not staying on at school.

Behaviour
Behavioural issues also impacted on Traveller students' retention in secondary school, leading to, in some instances, their exclusion (official and unofficial) from school, which led to further dis-

engagement and ultimately withdrawal for a number of students in the study. Behavioural issues were only a factor for the boys who dropped out of school, with over half of them experiencing behavioural problems in school, including four who were given fixed-term exclusions and one who was permanently excluded (see Appendix 4). TES staff felt that schools sometimes excluded Traveller students because they did not have the support networks to cope with their difficulties: 'a lot of schools will say 'well there is nobody to help or advise us we will put them out until somebody does come' (TES teacher). Once students are excluded from school the likelihood of successful reintegration significantly deteriorates. TES staff raised concerns about the support networks available to all students, including Traveller students, with behavioural difficulties in school. Students had to 'fail' and then wait for support, there was no immediate intervention which might prevent exclusion: 'no one hands-on that could react really quickly and save that kid ... if they could just nip it in the bud quicker it would save a lot of grief' (TES teacher). The low expectations of school staff regarding Traveller students' behaviour meant that some students, like Matthew, conformed to such expectations.

Racism and bullying

Issues of racism and bullying may play a part in Traveller students' withdrawal from school. For many Traveller students behavioural issues within school arose from their retaliation to racist name-calling. However, parents and students' mechanisms for dealing with such name-calling or injustices within the school were often at odds with the behaviour expected so Traveller students were punished for 'hitting back'. This was an issue for Glyn, Matthew and Billy in particular. There were incidents when Traveller students' retaliation to racial bullying led to their exclusion:

> He were getting bullied at school ... So Matthew got mad one day and ... when he chucked the lad down the steps he got excluded for it. The other lad didn't get excluded (Matthew's mother).

> He got into trouble for fighting back all the time. It's just something that they do, they just won't take no messing ... they won't let people call them names (Glyn's mother).

Even Peter, who generally had no behavioural problems in school, was excluded for retaliating to racist name-calling. Although teachers may have empathised with their response, they were unable to condone their behaviour. Cultural norms regarding behaviour were problematic because many Traveller parents felt that their children should retaliate and this clashed with cultural norms within school. Matthew's mother said that in a meeting about her son's exclusion a senior member of school staff had said:

> If you're going to turn round and say that you condone Matthew's fighting in the classroom he can never come back to this school at all. Well I daren't say what I felt; I daren't say I think he did right thing.

As she went on to observe:

> How can you tell a Travelling kid that the best man walks away? The best man doesn't walk away ... if you walk away you're the laughing stock of the whole country; it's bred in them. 'Cos if their dad walked away he'd never be able to walk again.

Racial bullying and name-calling may have been a factor in the withdrawal of students in the study; for Louisa and Seamus it played a part in their non-transfer to secondary school. Both had been bullied quite severely at primary school, resulting in Seamus not attending school for a number of years and Louisa changing primary schools and hiding her cultural identity in her new primary school. Students' and parents' fears regarding a resurgence in racial bullying at secondary school may have influenced their non-transfer.

Sometimes racial incidents at school were seen as a catalyst for withdrawal. For example, when a serious incident occurred in Year 7 between Traveller and non-Traveller students, Ross and Ryan's mother removed them from school because she was worried about retaliation against them, even though they were not involved in the original incident. Similarly, Glyn's mother felt she had to remove him from school because 'there was too much prejudice and ... fighting'. Christopher attended the same school as Glyn and his mother's fears regarding her son's safety resulted in her withdrawing him from school as well:

> There was an incident of racial trouble where there was quite a big fight, Christopher wasn't involved ... but after that Mum said Christopher wasn't ever coming back to school. She was ... worried for his safety (head of Year 9).

The TES teacher observed that the level of racial conflict within the school meant that Traveller students had to 'stick together' to protect themselves.

Relationships and liaison

Breakdown in relationships or lack of liaison between home and school may have led to the withdrawal of some students. In some cases good relationships were never established with the secondary schools so it was difficult to address problems students were having if there was no dialogue with parents. Louis' secondary school observed that his 'parents were very reluctant to come into school', in contrast to his primary school where the TES teacher described the home school relationship as 'brilliant and it doesn't involve me'.

For two students who did not transfer, Louisa and Bernie, poor communication and awareness regarding which secondary school they were transferring to may have accounted for their non-transfer. In some instances there was also a feeling from schools that parents were waiting for an incident to happen so that they could remove their children from school 'any incidents that happened within school were just ammunition to take them out really' (head of year). Conversely, parents also expressed frustration at schools' exclusion of Traveller children because that was what they wanted:

> You're throwing him out of the school and he's loving it, you're just doing him a favour. So they [the school] stopped doing it then. I told them 'I've got such a hard job to make him go to school and when I do you throw him out again' (Glyn's mother).

Size of school

Disengaged youngsters, when describing their dislocation from school, often focus on the size, ethos and atmosphere of secondary schools, with many wanting to return to the smaller, 'safer', primary school context, which they view in a more positive light (Kinder *et al*, 1999). These factors were also raised by interviewees as having a detrimental impact on the retention of some Traveller students in this study. For example, both Ronnie and Nick had 'begged' their TES teacher to let them return to primary school and when interviewed Ronnie asked: 'Can't you put me into that little school again? The little school's better'. Both Ronnie and Nick were intimidated by the size of their secondary school. Ronnie said: 'It's too big ... the little school like you didn't have to go for miles for a class'. Similarly, Nick was 'hugely intimidated' by the secondary school building and had said that it was 'a bad place ... the corridors are too long' (TES teacher).

Analysis across the group of students who did not complete Key Stage 3 found that nearly half had attended larger secondary schools.

Table 7.1 Size of school attended by students who dropped out

Size of school	Number of students who dropped out
Small (less than 750 students)	3
Medium (between 750 – 1100)	6
Large (over 1100)	8

School performance

In terms of school performance, analysis of the DfES schools standards performance data (2002) showed that more than half (eleven) transferred to schools where performance exceeded the local and national average. The remaining seven students transferred to schools that performed below the LEA and national average (including two schools that were well below average).

The 'culture shock' of transferring to secondary school for many students is well documented. However, for some Traveller students in the study, it was seen as too great, particularly those with low levels of literacy:

> These kids, some of which are emerging readers, suddenly have no reading scheme, they are herded about in a system that's alien to them (TES teacher).

Students' cultural isolation within the secondary school context might also have influenced their withdrawal. Ronnie, who attended a primary school with a large proportion of Traveller students and only tended to associate with Traveller students, found himself at secondary school with no other Traveller students in his form group. The lack of social and cultural support within this context meant that he found it particularly difficult to integrate:

> There was no good friends there; I'm in a big class by meself. They [Traveller friends] was in my class all the time at little school and in the big school we had to split apart.

The size of secondary schools was also linked to cultural fears Traveller parents held about secondary education in general. Smaller schools were seen as 'good' and larger schools as 'bad', although one of the largest secondary schools in the sample had a good record of retaining Traveller students. Nevertheless, school and TES interviewees in two LEAs felt that the previous existence of smaller middle schools had aided the retention of Traveller students because the size and ethos of the schools, along with the age of the students attending, meant that they were more like primary schools.

Points for reflection

- How are schools addressing the statutory requirement to audit and review all policies in the light of the RRAA and assess their impact on Gypsy Traveller students?

- Given the behavioural issues and relationship difficulties exhibited by some Traveller students who were not retained in secondary school, is there the need for additional nurturing, mentoring and support networks within schools which can be accessed swiftly to address students' needs? Could TES teaching assistants or an identified member of the school staff be identified to formalise this role?

- Parental attitudes as well as cultural influences and expectations clearly have a significant impact on Traveller students' retention within secondary school. Would additional school and TES focused home/school liaison improve both schools' and parents' awareness and acceptance of both a Traveller and school-based education? Would additional links with fathers, as most links are with mothers, focusing on the benefits of a school-based education be effective?

- Would an identified contact person in school for Traveller parents aid dialogue and help keep channels of communication open, when the home/school relationship becomes strained?

- Would data monitoring which analysed the links between attainment, attendance and behaviour ensure the most effective targeting of support?

- Do schools need to explore and increase their understanding of the reasons behind Traveller students' behaviour, such as their response to racist name-calling, and to implement strategies which focus on conflict resolution?

- Do expectations of Traveller students' attainment, behaviour and attendance need to be raised in order for students to stay in secondary school?

- Do schools have clear guidelines regarding 'core values' and 'respect' and do they treat Traveller students as individuals, rather than defining them by their ethnicity?

- Do schools take responsibility and ownership for all their students reflected in strong policies on inclusion, low rates of permanent exclusion and do they have strategies focusing on alternatives to exclusion? Do they make Traveller students feel valued and do they value a Traveller education? Do they have strong pastoral systems and clear induction programmes for students entering the school during the course of the year?

- Do schools need to be able and willing to adapt, differentiate and diversify the curriculum, where appropriate, by providing alternative packages focusing on work-related learning and college placements, in order to retain students? Would vocational options, which incorporate Traveller trades, develop skills that are culturally valuable, whilst continuing with a school education?

8

Keeping on track

The focus of this chapter is the group of twenty students who completed Key Stage 3. Four case studies are provided at the beginning of the chapter to give a flavour of the background and experiences of some of these 'retained' students. Each case study includes a number of possible factors that may be associated with their successful retention in secondary education. These factors are then explored in more depth using componential analysis to see whether any commonality or pattern can be discerned across the 'retained' group of students. Finally, comparisons are made between the two groups (of retained and non-retained students) to help identify or eliminate possible associations.

An examination of factors which might be associated with retention in secondary school

Each of the four case studies provides a list of possible factors which might be associated with successful retention through Key Stage 3. These factors will now be examined in turn, to determine whether any patterns emerged across the cohort of twenty retained students.

Parental attitudes

Interviews with parents were analysed in order to ascertain their views on the value of secondary education. The table in Appendix 1 shows how influential parental views could be in predicting the likelihood of student retention and drop-out (38 per cent of the

Case study 1 Shelley

Shelley was the youngest of three children and lived on a private plot in a rural location. Her older brother and sister had both attended secondary school until Year 11. Dad had been to secondary school but mum had not and was not literate. Shelley had previously attended a small primary school with approximately 15 per cent Traveller students. She had no gaps in her education and transferred to a secondary school several miles from her home. A school bus picked her up and dropped her off outside her gate. The school was large, with over 1400 students, and between 30 and 50 Traveller students on roll (including several housed Travellers). Shelley was proud of her identity but mixed predominantly with Non-Traveller peers. She socialised with her friends in the evenings and at weekends.

Shelley was described as mature, popular, articulate and hard-working. Her primary school teachers predicted her to be 'head girl material'. She was absent during the week of Key Stage 2 SATs but teacher predictions placed her at Level 4 across the board. She was predicted to achieve Levels 5-6 at Key Stage 3 and at least 5 A-Cs at GCSE. Shelley's attendance was described as 'very good' in primary school and averaged over 90 per cent in Year 7. Her attendance dipped in Year 8 but then improved in Year 9 (averaging 75 per cent).

Shelley took a full and active part in extra-curricular activities, including school trips. In Year 6 she was allowed to take part in a residential week away. Her parents were supportive of education and her mum wanted her to have the chances she herself did not get. Shelley had no direct support from the TES in school but there was continuity of support personnel between the primary and secondary phase. A young Traveller LSA set up some successful initiatives in the secondary school and Shelley became involved in a couple of groups targeted at Traveller students. Shelley used Romani words and said that she had not experienced racism at school. Shelley had ambitions to train as a midwife.

Possible factors

- Siblings with positive experience of secondary school
- School with experience and knowledge of Travellers
- Easy access to school (home to school journey)
- Secure about cultural identity
- Secure social network (Travellers and gaujes)
- Good interpersonal skills
- No problems accessing the curriculum
- Regular attendance
- Uninterrupted pattern of schooling
- Involvement in extra–curricular activities
- Positive role model in school (Traveller LSA)
- No experience of racism
- High aspirations
- Positive parental attitudes

Case Study 2 Danny

Danny was the second oldest of four children and lived on a private plot on the outskirts of a city. His older brother attended secondary school until Year 11. Neither of his parents had been to secondary school themselves and did not read or write. Danny had attended the local infant school and Church of England junior school, both serving an area of social deprivation and with Travellers representing just under 10 per cent of the roll. However, there was no history of secondary transfer and Danny's brother was the only one to transfer. Danny transferred to the same small secondary school with less than 500 students. The school had been found to have serious weaknesses but was improving. Like the primary school, the secondary school served a socially deprived catchment. Unlike the primary school, it had very little experience of Traveller students. Danny's parents drove him to and from school. Although there were many other Travellers living in the same area, Danny's family set themselves apart. His parents described the behaviour of local Traveller children as anti-social and they discouraged any form of contact. Danny and his parents were open about their heritage but perceived themselves to be different from these other Travellers. Members of Danny's extended family were against secondary education.

Danny was described by his teachers as popular, hard-working, confident and eager to please. There was never any doubt in the minds of his primary teachers that he would transfer. His achievement at the end of Key Stage 2 was below national expectations (Levels 2-3), although his reading age was above his chronological age. Danny was not on the SEN register. In secondary school, Danny was perceived as a good achiever in relation to his peers and was predicted Levels 4-5 at the end of Key Stage 3. His attendance had always been very good, averaging over 90 per cent. His behaviour was excellent and he had not had a detention in Key Stage 3.

Danny was a keen footballer and had always played for the school team in both primary and secondary schools. He was not, however, permitted to participate in residential trips. His mother described herself as over-protective. His parents attended parents' evenings and were very supportive of the school. Danny had no direct support from the TES in school, although his mother had a good relationship with the fieldworker who had supported the family over a number of years. All his school friends were non-Travellers, apart from one 'half-Traveller' friend with whom he sometimes spoke Romani. Danny said that he rarely encountered any form of racial harassment in school. Danny had no clear vocational ambition although he loved football and drama. There was an expectation in the family that he would go into a family business with one of his uncles, although Danny wasn't sure that this was what he wanted to do.

Possible factors

- Sibling with positive experience of secondary school
- Small secondary school
- Positive parental attitudes
- Non–association with those who give Travellers a 'bad name'
- Good interpersonal skills
- Secure social network (Travellers and *gaujes*)
- Regular attendance
- Uninterrupted pattern of schooling
- Achieves well in relation to ability
- Involvement in extra–curricula activities
- Little experience of racism in school

Case study 3 Kizzy

Kizzy's parents were divorced when she was younger and during the course of the study she lived in a house in a large city with her father, step-mother (non-Traveller) and younger step-brother and sister. Kizzy's dad had not been to secondary school, although her step-mother had. Kizzy's dad was supportive of secondary education up to a point but members of the extended family were against the idea and he had echoed their views. Her step-mum thought that Traveller attitudes about education were resistant to change but she felt that her husband was beginning to recognise the benefits. Kizzy did not start primary school until the age of seven and then moved to a different area and school the following year. She moved again and started another primary school in Year 6 after a period out of school, pending an appeal. There were three other Traveller students at the school. Her step-mother felt that Kizzy fitted in with both cultures and did not feel excluded in any way. Kizzy attended a summer school at the end of Year 6 and transferred to the local secondary school, which was within walking distance. The school had a very difficult inner city catchment. It had approximately 700 students on roll but only five other Traveller students, including a cousin. Kizzy kept her Traveller identity hidden at school. All her friends in school were non-Travellers.

Despite gaps in her education, Kizzy settled well in primary school. Kizzy's cultural identity was not generally known. She was described as popular, motivated and happy. The headteacher said she had excellent social skills and was very well-adjusted. She took part in a residential trip and her father was always there at class assemblies. Parents also attended parents' evenings. She achieved Level 4s and a Level 5 in science at the end of Key Stage 2. Key Stage 3 predictions were Level 5s in maths and English and Level 4 in science and she attended SATs booster classes in Year 9. Her attendance was good in both primary school and secondary (averaging over 90 per cent).

Kizzy took part in a wide range of extra-curricular activities. Although Kizzy had no in-school support, TES provided support in accessing a primary school place and continued to monitor attendance and achievement in secondary school. Kizzy had consistently had high aspirations for a professional, caring career such as nursing, teaching or social work.

In Year 9, Kizzy's step-mother left the family.

Possible factors

- Influence of non-Traveller step–mother
- High academic ability reduced effect of disrupted education
- Additional support, such as summer school and booster classes
- Easy access to school
- 'Passing' of cultural identity
- No experience of racism
- Good interpersonal skills
- Secure social network (gauje)
- High aspirations
- Regular attendance
- Involvement in extra-curricular activities

Case Study 4 Charlie

Charlie lived on local authority Traveller site in an urban area with his mother and younger brother and sister. Charlie also had an older brother who had been to secondary school. Charlie's mum could not read but his grandmother could. Charlie went to a primary school with a large proportion of Traveller students but made little progress there and was subjected to racist name-calling. There were also altercations between Traveller families. Subsequently, when Charlie was ten, his mother and a neighbour moved all their children to a different school which had no history of admitting Travellers. Charlie had a hearing and visual impairment and had to attend hospital appointments. These sensory impairments were not obvious to his teachers, although his learning delay was eventually recognised and he was placed on stage 3 of the SEN code of practice and received LSA support. No support from TES was provided. Charlie transferred to a local secondary school with around 800 students which was a mile away, with one other Traveller friend. They were the only Travellers on roll at the time, although the school had a history of housed Traveller students. Charlie had a wide group of friends, both Traveller and *gaujes* with whom he socialised outside school.

Charlie was highly regarded by staff and peers in his second primary school. Despite literacy problems, he was highly articulate and had good general knowledge. He was considered to be functioning at Levels 3-4 at the end of Key Stage 2. In secondary school he received additional in-class support from school and the TES and was moved down from School Action Plus to School Action because of his progress. He was predicted Level 4s in English and Science and possibly Level 5 in Maths. Charlie was described by secondary school teachers as a mature boy with an excellent attitude. He was elected Form Representative and Boy's Representative in Year 7.

He played regularly for the school football team and took part in extra-curricular activities, including a residential school trip. Charlie's attendance was consistently good, over 90 per cent. Apart from his early experiences in primary school, Charlie did not report any further name-calling or racial harassment. He had a good group of friends, including the Traveller student who lived on the same site, and who transferred with him. This friend left school half-way through Year 8, opting for Education Otherwise. This unsettled Charlie and he said that school was less appealing since his friend left. He expected to complete Year 11 and then follow a traditional Traveller occupation such as tree work, like his father.

Possible factors

- Older sibling transferred to secondary school
- Additional support for recognised SEN
- Secondary school within walking distance
- Secure friendship network (Traveller and *gauje*)
- Good interpersonal skills
- Participation in extra–curricula activities
- Regular attendance
- No subjection to racism

parents correctly predicted that their children would be out of school before the end of Key Stage 3).

Analysis of the parent interviews from the retained group revealed that the majority of parents (fourteen out of twenty) made statements that reflected a high value attached to secondary education. These parents said they hoped that their children would be successful in their exams and go on to college or get a 'good job'. The parents of the boys were determined that their sons should complete their education, although only one mentioned aspirations for higher education and a professional career. The girls' mothers spoke about college (and even university) and used the term 'career' when considering vocational routes. These mothers also made reference to the fact that they wanted their daughters to have more chances and choices in life than they'd had themselves: 'I want her to go to college and experience all the things that I missed out on'. A number of the parents said that the traditional Traveller lifestyle was dying out and that education was essential for the next generation 'you can't pretend it's not important anymore'.

It is interesting to note that these positive attitudes were expressed by parents who had not been to secondary school themselves. Of the fourteen mothers, only two had attended a secondary school: the others said they were unable to read and write.

The remaining six parents presented mixed views or intimated that their children might leave school before the end of Year 11. There was an implication here that the decision would be left up to their sons and daughters.

> I'm hoping he'll follow school right through but it depends on him basically. I'm not as confident now that I'll get him right through to finishing.

> The day she says I'd rather stay at home and learn to cook proper and everything that's the day I say 'you stay at home then because if you don't think you're learning anything and I don't think you're learning anything I think it's a waste of time you going'.

> I hope he'll sit his exams but I'm not going to badger him.

When compared with parental views from the non-retained group, there is quite a stark difference. Of the seventeen parents in this group who expressed an opinion, only two had made statements that reflected a high value on education. Two others presented mixed opinions and thirteen saw little worth in secondary education. These parents tended to hold traditional views on gender roles and saw literacy as the important educational goal.

> I'd be looking for him to be a better reader and writer because when he's 15 he'll want to go out and do something to earn money for himself.

> She's learnt what I wanted her to learn do you know what I mean? I mean she's a good reader and a good writer and she can write a letter. She can do what I want her to do, she can do a lot, she can do a lot more than what her dad can do. She's done what I wanted her to do.

This is strong evidence that parental attitudes are associated with student retention.

Siblings' experience at secondary school

Shelley, Danny and Charlie all had older siblings at secondary school. Kizzy, on the other hand, was the eldest child in her family and was therefore the first to transfer. Shelley and Danny both had brothers a couple of years older than themselves, who went to the same school and who had settled well, without any major problems. The gap between Charlie and his brother was greater and when Charlie transferred, his older brother had already left school. Although it was not confirmed whether his brother had left before statutory leaving age, Charlie benefited from the experience because he was befriended by older students who had known his brother.

Analysis across the whole cohort of retained students (20) shows that three-fifths of the students (12) had older siblings who had attended secondary school. In the majority of these cases, sibling experiences had been described as positive, with older brothers and sisters continuing through to statutory school leaving age. In three cases, however, sibling experiences of secondary school had been less than satisfactory, resulting in early drop-out.

When compared to the cohort who left school before the end of Key Stage 3, a slightly smaller proportion of the children, half of them, had older brothers or sisters who transferred to secondary school.

However, the quality of the experience and length of time that siblings were in secondary school seemed to be a more important factor than the success of transfer, so that positive school experiences of siblings were much more common amongst the retained children in the sample than amongst those who left school. In this way, parent, student and teacher attitudes may be positively influenced, leading to higher expectations from all concerned. One TES teacher described this process as 'echoing down'. Older siblings perhaps provided the only positive role model for students. (Apart from one case, there were no adult Travellers working in the secondary schools). The pattern of confrontational or unhappy experiences of secondary school tended to be repeated within families. What is unclear is whether this pattern was due to family or school expectations, or a combination of both.

Nearly half of the students, eight of them were, like Kizzy, the oldest in their families and therefore the first to transfer to secondary school. When compared to those students who did not complete Key Stage 3, there is very little difference in the two groups. Students who were the first in their families to transfer were just as likely to stay on as they were to leave.

Size of school

Danny transferred to a small secondary school with less than 500 students on roll. Interviews with Danny and his parents revealed that this was a positive and helpful factor in their view. Analysis across the group of retained students found that although more students in this group did attend the smaller secondary schools, results were not particularly consistent, as the table below illustrates:

Table 8.1

Size of school	Number of students in the retained group
Small (less than 750 students)	9
Medium (between 750-1100)	6
Large (over 1100)	7

NB: *Total does not add up 20 because three students transferred elsewhere during Key Stage 3 and two of the schools had more than one retained student.*

School performance

According to DfES schools standards performance data (2002) neither was there a clear pattern in relation to Key Stage 3 and GCSE results achieved by the schools that these retained students attended.

- seven students attended schools that performed better than the LEA and national average

- two attended schools that performed in line with the LEA and national average

- ten attended schools that performed below LEA and national average, including four schools that were well below average

- one school was a special school and therefore N/A.

However, of the group who dropped out of school during Key Stage 3, more than half (ten out of eighteen) transferred to schools where performance exceeded the local and national average. This suggests that Traveller students are accessing high performing schools but that their needs are not being sufficiently met there.

Schools with experience of Travellers

The school attended by Shelley, and also by Leanne and Joe, had a long history of admitting Traveller students. In recent years levels of retention had risen, with more Traveller students staying on until statutory leaving age. The headteacher put this shift down to two main factors: a more sedentary lifestyle being adopted by the local Traveller community and the school's approach to meeting individual student needs. The TES had been involved in staff development initiatives and a young Traveller LSA was based part-time in the school. In addition, the school's senior management team included a former TES co-ordinator who brought a wealth of specialist expertise.

To what extent was this example typical of the other schools which retained students? Analysis revealed that only two other schools had an established pattern or history of admitting Traveller students. One of these was also successful at retaining students to Year 11, whereas the other had retention difficulties. However, the two students who initially transferred to these schools subsequently left to go elsewhere. In one case, the family moved to a different authority and in the other, the student moved to a special school. All the other schools attended by the retained students were relatively inexperienced in dealing with Traveller students.

The data also show no apparent links between the likelihood of retention and the number of other Traveller students on roll. Of those students who did complete Key Stage 3, seven (more than a third) transferred to schools where they were the only Traveller student in their year group

The data here suggests, that the pedigree of a school, in terms of its history and experience of admitting Traveller students may not be a factor associated with retention. Generally speaking, levels of awareness about Traveller culture in the secondary schools were low, as evidenced by interviews with students, parents and TES personnel. Three of the schools showed a reluctance to take up TES offers of INSET. Interviews with TES staff suggested that the attitude of individual teachers or heads of year was perhaps a more important factor in relation to retention. The style of leadership and ethos were also important considerations. The headteachers of the two schools which had the most success with retaining Traveller students both emphasised that they were good at retaining students generally, not just Travellers. Both heads spoke passionately about inclusion and their reluctance to exclude any student.

Cultural identity

> To be successful at secondary school, [a Traveller student] must have the character to stand out and be different and have sufficient resilience to cope with the knocks that come because you are different ... and to cope with many adults who are biased (Year 6 class teacher).

This primary school teacher postulated that successful retention in secondary school could depend upon a student's ability to assert their cultural identity positively and to have the resilience to deal with racism and alienation. Members of minority groups adopt different strategies for survival in majority culture including 'passing' or hiding their identity. The strategy described above, bears a resemblance to what Shain, (2003) called 'resistance through culture.' Shain found that Asian girls who adopted this strategy were more likely to have negative relations with staff, complain of being misunderstood and unfairly treated, play truant and have lower expectations of academic success. These factors were more characteristic of Traveller students in the current study who left before the end of Key Stage 3, than of the retained group.

Shelley was open about her identity at school. She joined clubs and groups which were targeted at young Travellers and said that she shared her knowledge of Romani with her *gauje* friends. She mixed well with both Travellers and non-Travellers and took a full and active part in school life. She had high aspirations for a professional career. This suggests a secure sense of identity or acculturation. Was this approach typical of the other nineteen students who completed Key Stage 3?

Seven of them, Leanne, Crystal, Helena, Marie, Joe, Charlie and Kieran showed similar characteristics. These students were also open about their identity and made no attempt to hide or deny their heritage. All seven of these students socialised with *gauje* friends out of school and visited one another's homes. There was also an apparent willingness to use Romani or Gammon words in the presence of non-Travellers.

Kenny, Dean and Kimberley also made no attempt to hide their identities. However, these students complained about the prevalence of racist name-calling in school. Their response tended to be aggressive and their behaviour was thus perceived to be challenging. All three students had a history of relationship difficulties with peers.

Danny, Eileen, Gemma, David, Shane, and Bridget were more guarded about disclosing their identities in school. These students were open with their friends but did not always trust the reaction of others. In some cases past experience of racial bullying may have led to this defence mechanism. In other cases students seemed anxious about being associated with local Travellers who were seen to reinforce negative stereotypes. These students seemed less prepared to divulge, share or discuss their use of Romani or Gammon.

Chelsea, Becky and Kizzy said they chose to 'pass', concealing or even denying their cultural identity.

This analysis suggests that individuals adopt different coping strategies which work for them. However, of the twenty that were retained in school, two-fifths (eight) appeared to co-exist confidently and comfortably within and between the two cultures.

Social networks

In each of the four case studies presented, students were described as having strong friendship networks in school. According to their teachers, in both primary and secondary school, these four students were popular with their peers. They related well to boys and girls and maintained a circle of mainly *gauje* friends with whom they socialised out of school. These students made new friends quite easily but also spoke of long-standing relationships which had been sustained over a number of years.

This pattern was repeated in the case of six other students in the retained group. Therefore, half the students (ten) who completed Key Stage 3 appeared to have a secure social network of friends in school. Not surprisingly, this group included all eight of those perceived to have a secure cultural identity. Of the ten students who apparently related less well with their peers, four had become increasingly socially isolated since transferring to secondary school and six had experienced some difficulties in their relationships with peers since primary school.

In comparison with the 24 students who did not complete Key Stage 3, there are some similarities and some differences. The same number of students (ten) were said to be popular and well-integrated in school until the point at which they left. However, three times as many students (twelve as opposed to four) were perceived to become increasingly isolated as they progressed into secondary education. These students were also characterised by increasingly sporadic attendance and a weak identification with the majority culture, including limited contact with non-Traveller children out of school.

Students' interpersonal skills and qualities

The ability to relate successfully to peers may well be linked to effective interpersonal skills. Ability in this area of personal effectiveness may also help students in their interaction with staff and reduce the likelihood of conflict. Interviews with school and TES staff were therefore analysed for evidence about students' interpersonal skills. Of the twenty students in the retained group, almost three-quarters (fourteen) were noted for their good interpersonal skills and were perceived by their teachers to demonstrate the following qualities:

- politeness (11)
- a mature attitude (8)
- articulacy (8)
- good sense of humour (7)
- willingness to help others (5)
- good team player (4)
- modesty (3)
- assertiveness (2)
- good listening skills (2)
- tolerance (1)

Attendance

As shown in Chapter 3, three-quarters of the students in the sample were identified as having attendance problems at some point during Key Stage 3. This included half of the students in the retained group.

Of the twenty students who completed Key Stage 3:

- four achieved average attendance of over 90 per cent
- six achieved average attendance of between 80-90 per cent
- nine achieved average attendance of between 60-80 per cent
- one achieved average attendance of between 50-60 per cent.

Where attendance was identified as a cause for concern, teachers drew attention to its impact on their attainment and their relationships with peers. In two cases, poor attendance was attributed mainly to medical reasons, in one case it was thought to be related to difficult circumstances at home and another was due to behaviour difficulties and a breakdown of home-school relationships. The six remaining students had a pattern of casual absence, which was being monitored.

From the data available, average attendance for the non-retained group was as follows:

- two achieved average attendance of over 90 per cent
- two achieved average attendance of between 80-90 per cent
- five achieved average attendance of between 60-80 per cent

- one achieved average attendance of between 50-60 per cent
- six achieved average attendance of less than 50 per cent.

These two sets of results are not strictly comparable, as the latter group may have been affected by complications surrounding the removal of students from the school roll. However, the comparison shows that the retained group contained more students with higher attendance rates.

Patterns of schooling

Kizzy was said to be achieving well in school, despite the fact that she had a disrupted pattern of schooling. She was not presented for school until the age of seven and then attended three different primary schools before transferring to secondary. During this period, she also spent several months out of school during an appeal. Her teachers described her as 'bright and able' and her attainment was in line with, and even exceeded, national averages by the end of Key Stage 2. Kizzy had achieved well despite an interrupted start to her education. Were there other examples of students achieving against the odds, or was this an isolated case?

An examination of the data identified that the pattern of schooling for the other nineteen retained students was varied. Apart from Kizzy, Eileen was the only other student in the group to be presented late for school. Eileen started primary school half way through Key Stage 1. All others had an uninterrupted education and several went to pre-school provision before the age of five.

Two students, Shane and Becky, also had fairly disrupted patterns of schooling. Both had attended more than one primary school and two secondary schools each. This pattern was due to their families moving from one area to another. Shane started a new school in a different authority in Year 9. When the family moved again shortly afterwards, his mother decided to transport him rather than change to a third secondary school.

Eileen and Dean had a settled primary school experience but then changed schools in Key Stage 3. In Eileen's case, this decision, taken shortly after transfer, was of her own making as she missed her best friend and wanted to be at the same school. Dean had specific learning difficulties and transferred to a special school which was more able to meet his needs.

Nearly half the students (eight) had attended more than one primary school. Some students, like Kimberley and Kieran, had apparently attended several different schools. It was difficult to obtain reliable data because parents were not always specific and primary school headteachers often had no reliable information about previous school history.

However, the remaining eight students had a very stable pattern of schooling, attending only one feeder primary from the age of five and one secondary school. Only three of these students were housed, the others lived on local authority or private sites. One student in this group lived on an unauthorised site.

Although this analysis provides an interesting insight, it should be remembered that the sample for the research was drawn from children who had been relatively 'settled' in the educational sense. The experiences of the non-retained group therefore reflect a similar pattern of experiences. However, as this study has identified, a settled lifestyle in itself does not necessarily guarantee a Traveller student's retention in secondary school.

Access to school (home to school journey)

Transport difficulties and problems relating to distance are often perceived as barriers preventing Traveller students from going to school. Was the distance between home and school a factor that might influence retention? How did the students who completed Key Stage 3 get to and from school? Although Shelley lived four miles from her school, a school bus picked her up from just outside her gate. Analysis across the group of twenty retained students found that the students were just as likely to live locally and within walking distance as they were to live further afield. Two students lived more than eight miles away from school. Dean went to a special school within the authority for which transport was provided. Shane's mother, however, made a 40 mile round trip each day to enable her children to maintain educational continuity. In response to this level of commitment, the TES made a contribution by off-setting the cost of petrol expenses.

The data showed that:

- ten students lived within two miles of their school
- four students lived between two and three miles away
- four students lived between three and five miles away
- two students lived between eight and eleven miles away.

Three other students travelled to school and back by bus. Joe caught a school bus for his five-mile journey but this stopped in the village (a ten-minute walk away) and was often late. Chelsea said the same about her school bus. The third student, Becky had experienced problems with bullying on the journey to and from school. Leanne was provided with a taxi as she lived five miles away and had a statement for SEN.

Of the group of students who left during Key Stage 3, it emerged that five students were provided with taxis to and from school, four caught buses, three lived within a mile and walked and one student who was on a part-time timetable was driven to school by the TES teacher.

These data suggest that half the retained students lived within walking distance of their schools. Other students travelled considerable distances to access school, including four who travelled on buses. However, in five cases the provision of a taxi did not help to retain students.

Access to the curriculum

Shelley, Kizzy and Danny were perceived by their teachers to have no difficulty in accessing the curriculum. Charlie presented with signs of learning delay, due to either sensory impairment and/or a negative experience of primary education. He was eventually placed on stage 3 of the SEN register when he changed primary schools in Year 6. In secondary school, he received additional learning support and was moved down a stage to 'School Action' in Year 9. Ability to access the curriculum may therefore be a factor which encourages retention.

When the 38 students transferred to secondary school, seventeen of them were found to be on the SEN register. By Year 8 this figure had risen to nineteen. This represents 50 per cent and is hugely disproportionate when compared to the general population. One of the additional students had no particular learning or behavioural needs but was placed at stage 1 'just so people would be aware of her', whereas the other student's behavioural difficulties were identified. In one other case there was some confusion in that the SENCO believed that external support from the TES should automatically place a Traveller student at stage 3 of the code of practice.

Of the students who completed Key Stage 3, half (ten) had been identified as having special needs. By this time, the Code of Practice had been revised and there was no longer a requirement for schools to maintain a register of SEN but most SENCOs still made reference to this. Both students with statements for SEN completed Key Stage 3. One, Dean, transferred to a special school and the other, Leanne, was making progress and achieving Level 4 in some areas of the curriculum in Year 9. This suggests that at least half the students who completed Key Stage 3 had some additional learning support.

However, just under half the students with identified learning difficulties (nine) did not stay in the school system, although one continued with home tuition. Therefore, the proportion of students with SEN was similar for both groups, even though the overall picture was one of disproportionate representation. When compared with the population as a whole, the students in this study achieved levels of attainment which were lower than national expectations at both Key Stages. This analysis suggests there are no apparent links between retention and student ability, although the level and nature of curriculum support are important features.

Extra-curricular involvement

Each of the four students in the case studies took part in a range of extra-curricular activities. Shelley was actively involved in two different groups targeted at Traveller students, as well as several sports activities. Danny and Charlie regularly represented their schools at football throughout Key Stage 3, while Kizzy was involved in drama productions and the school choir.

A clear pattern emerged when the experiences of the other students were examined. Of the retained group, all but five students (Joe, Eileen, Kimberley, Bridget and Chelsea) took part in secondary school clubs or activities. In other words, three-quarters of the re-tained students were involved in this way. Of the non-retained group, only three students (Glyn, Christopher and Peter) took part in extra-curricula activities in secondary school. This means that the vast majority of students (nearly five out of six) who were not retained, took no part in extra-curricula activities. This finding suggests an association between participation and retention.

Experience of racism

Shelley maintained throughout the study that she was not subjected to racism at school, although this was not a typical response across the sample. Only a quarter of the students (five) in the retained group expressed this view. This group comprised three girls and two boys. Of those who were asked in the leaver's group, only two students (13 per cent) said that they had not encountered racism at school. This finding confirms that most, but not all Traveller students said they had encountered racism in school.

Points for reflection

- Parental attitudes are clearly an important factor in school retention. The mothers of the retained students believed that secondary education was important because it promised to offer more choice and opportunity for their children. Could more be done to confirm and reinforce this idea through proactive and imaginative work with parents?

- The employment of teaching assistants from the Traveller com-munity could provide more positive role models for students and help to promote the desirability of secondary education within the community.

- Are secondary schools addressing the issue of 'inclusion' through a clear programme of staff development, or is there an expectation that this 'ideal' will simply be taken on by staff? How do high performing schools meet the needs of a diverse population and promote inclusiveness effectively? Would aware-ness about Traveller culture be promoted more effectively as part of a wider, whole school training programme on inclusion?

- How can young Travellers best be supported during the development of their cultural identity? What opportunities are there for them to explore their cultural heritage with their contemporaries? Could LEAs support and facilitate the development of supplementary classes in which young Travellers learn about their language, history and culture from elders? This type of initiative, sometimes referred to as Saturday or supplementary provision, might also allay parental fears about the culture dying out and challenge the view that schools do not recognise the significance of Traveller culture.

- Would a secure network of friends help Traveller children to remain longer in school? A greater emphasis on the teaching of emotional literacy skills in both primary and secondary schools could help to equip all children in this way and promote qualities of tolerance, assertiveness and respect for oneself and others.

- Half of the students had been identified as having special educational needs. Although this was a purposive sample rather than a random selection, this appears to support other findings (Ofsted, 1996, 1999) about gross underachievement of Traveller students in secondary school. With so few students in most secondary schools, how can ethnic monitoring systems effectively pick up isolated and underachieving individuals? What more can be done to raise expectations?

- Retained students were more involved in extra-curricular activities than those who left school early. Students who take an active part in school life may feel more valued and included. Perhaps more could be done to encourage Traveller students to take part in extra-curricular activities?

- The experience of racism in school is a reality for many Traveller students. Is there an effective way of addressing this inherent problem in school? What opportunities are there for schools to share and disseminate good practice in this respect? What more could be done to break the cycle of racism-physical retaliation-punishment if Traveller students are taught to fight back in this way?

9

Conclusions

It is staggering how many of your original cohort are still in school. If you'd have done this [research] ten years ago, you'd have had nobody. (TES teacher)

Forty-four eleven-year-old Traveller students were identified. They agreed to take part in a unique longitudinal study that would follow their progress and experiences in Key Stage 3. In the event, thirty-eight of the students achieved the transfer to secondary schools and of those, twenty completed the first three years of secondary education. In other words, just under half of the original sample were retained in the school system to the age of fourteen. Although this finding raises obvious concern, it may also reflect an encouraging message when compared with earlier estimates that less than one in five Traveller students accessed school in Key Stage 3 (Ofsted, 1996). The quotation above shows that this study marks another step forward and illustrates how patterns and attitudes are gradually changing in relation to Traveller children and their engagement with secondary education.

Significantly, however, the students who took part in this study were largely sedentary and lived on established plots or in housing. Only three of the students lived on tolerated or unauthorised encampments. This focus on 'settled' Travellers was a deliberate feature of the research design but, had a larger and more representative sample of Travellers (including more mobile families) been considered, the findings might have revealed a less encouraging picture. The key message here is that engagement in secondary education can be precarious, whether a Traveller child lives in a house or on the roadside. This study provides insight into perceptions and experiences of the students and their parents, which may help to further our understanding of this complex issue. In this final chapter, an overview and summary of some key findings are presented under the broad headings of culture, identity and achievement.

Culture

Cultural influences clearly have an impact on the retention of Traveller students in secondary school. Traditionally, Traveller communities do not have a pattern of secondary school engagement, and adolescence is the time when young Traveller people are expected to help generate income or take on a wider range of domestic responsibilities. More than half of the parents who were interviewed expected their children to follow traditional and cultural gender-based roles and the children echoed their parents' aspirations. In many cases this incorporated the expectation of leaving school early and consequently over a third of the students transferred to secondary school with the understanding that this would be a temporary arrangement. Fifteen students and their parents correctly predicted at the age of 11 that they would be out of the school system by the age of 14.

The age at which childhood ends and adulthood begins is a fluid social and cultural construct. The raising of the school leaving to 16 and subsequent developments in education policy towards an increasingly academic curriculum over the past twenty years has effectively defined and consolidated this particular cultural boundary. Recent moves towards a more flexible and vocational curriculum at Key Stage 4 may help to mediate that boundary, although this may come too late for some students, if they leave the system before the end of Key Stage 3. Proportionately, boys were more likely than girls to drop out early and their withdrawal was often preceded by a breakdown in relationships between home and school. In a sense, it was as though the schools were 'on trial' and 'any incidents that happened ... were just ammunition to take them out' (head of year). When students were unhappy in school, parents were reluctant to make them attend. This was also found by Clay (1999). Amongst the parents of students who dropped out of school early, there was often a particularly weak affiliation with, or rejection of, *gauje* culture and values. There was an association between students who left school early and parents who expressed serious concern about sex education, or the potential negative influence of mainstream youth culture.

There was also evidence that traditional cultural attitudes and expectations were shifting. Primary schools and TESs reported an emerging pattern of successful transfer to secondary schools. Common factors associated with non-transfer were: late presentation for school late in Key Stage 1, parental attitudes which exhibited a rejection of majority culture and previous experiences of bullying. Several of the parents acknowledged that 'times had changed' and that Traveller communities could no longer rely on traditional patterns of employment. Just over a third of the mothers expressed hopes and aspirations for their children which challenged or diverged from traditional norms. Unsurprisingly, most of the parents of the retained students were in this group. Again, the children of this group echoed their parents' expectations. Over a third of the mothers in the sample spoke positively about the value of a secondary education and wanted their children to have more opportunity and choice than they themselves had experienced. Typically, these women were challenged by relatives, including partners and Traveller neighbours who interpreted their attitude as illogical or even cruel. Despite this pressure, a number of mothers seemed determined to make a stand and support the prospect of secondary education, and even further or higher education, as long as their children were happy and emotionally secure within that environment. Although a quarter of the children were not allowed to participate in residential visits or long day trips, an equal number had participated in outward bound activity holidays, including one school trip abroad.

Amongst all parents, the will or desire to keep aspects of the Traveller culture alive was evident. The vast majority of the students in the study said they had knowledge of and used a language at home in addition to English. Students and their parents described this as Romani, Gaelic or 'Traveller language' (Anglo-Romani or Gammon). Value placed on the maintenance of Gypsy Traveller customs and traditions was also apparent from interviews with students and their parents, regardless of whether they lived in houses or trailers. The majority of parents wanted their children to understand and be proud of their cultural heritage. Initiatives to celebrate Traveller culture were evident in primary schools but much less so in the secondary phase. However, it would appear that the adolescent Travellers, most of whom were isolated from Traveller peers in secondary school, were sensitive about this issue and did not want special attention for them or their culture in school. Most of the students attended secondary schools which were relatively inexperienced in their dealings with the Traveller community. The reasons for these findings may be related to adolescence and sensitivities surrounding the development of self-identity. It may also indicate the prevalence of racism and a primarily ethnocentric culture which permeates the education system.

Attempts to disentangle and identify the causes of secondary retention problems can focus too much on cultural explanations and lead to a theory of cultural pathology in which related factors may be overlooked or given insufficient attention. An example of this is where Traveller parent attitudes are seen to challenge or reject the values of the settled community. Protective behaviour, such as the refusal to allow a son or daughter to transfer to secondary school in the first place, may be interpreted as a conscious attempt by Traveller parents to restrict contact with *gauje* norms and values and to preserve their cultural identity by maintaining cultural boundaries. In reality, it may be a genuine fear or deep seated mistrust which underlies the decision. The majority of Traveller parents had not been through secondary school themselves. Those who had attended secondary school often spoke of negative experiences. It is hardly surprising that these parents expressed anxiety and concern for their children's well-being. Racism and bullying were what parents worried about most, followed by fears about drugs and moral welfare. The extent of this mistrust was illustrated by one student who said her mother had told her never to drink at school in case someone had tampered with it and laced it with drugs.

Three-quarters of the parents did not attend the secondary school parents' evenings. This may be interpreted by schools in cultural terms as a general lack of interest, relevance or support. However, interviews revealed that parents felt insecure and intimidated by the prospect of attending formal parents' evenings. The study also found that Traveller parents were generally compliant with school rules, even those conflicting with cultural customs such as the wearing of jewellery, if associated health and safety considerations were explained to them. Parents were less accepting of sanctions and punishments which they saw as unreasonable or unjustified. Relationships with teachers could then become strained by a mutually perceived lack of respect. This pattern was also evident amongst Traveller students who resented being shouted at by teachers and who would challenge perceived injustice. In some cases these situations led to dialogue, review and compromise. In others, however, it led to confrontation and the subsequent withdrawal of students.

Clearly, much more needs to be done to reduce the mutual suspicion between the two cultures. TES staff played an important role and were seen as cultural mediators but this role also brought about a number of tensions between schools and TES, mainly about misunderstandings of role expectations, the configuration of responsibilities and the 'ownership' of issues. Perhaps there needs to be a more open dialogue between schools and TESs about providing optimum support and working out the balance of reactive and proactive approaches.

Identity

The process of juggling and coming to terms with these sometimes conflicting sets of cultural expectations and norms has been described as cultural dissonance. Directives from parents to 'hit back' when bullied are known to contradict school expectations, invitations to interact socially with non-Traveller peers out of school and form friendships may be prohibited by parents who have negative perceptions of the majority culture, and vice versa. Exclusion from certain PHSE lessons, at the request of parents, may set students apart in school. Conversely, school expectations in relation to homework may be perceived as an unnecessary imposition which interferes with domestic chores and family life, and strict attendance policies may cause friction in the immediate and extended family. Schools may not always recognise the pressures some students are under to negotiate these competing cultural norms and values within a primarily ethnocentric school culture, or acknowledge their ability to operate successfully between different cultural contexts. Visions of 'inclusive schooling' therefore, need to take account of all the ways in which students can be disenfranchised, and how cultural norms and values are to be recognised.

Not only do students have to deal with cultural dissonance but most of them encountered racist incidents in school and felt alienated because they were usually the only Traveller in their class or year group. All these influences impact on students' development of identity and self-concept. Fundamentally, socio-psychocultural factors will shape a student's identity as a learner and will influence their educational experiences. Individuals who feel isolated, socially and culturally, are unlikely to reach their full potential.

Effects of racist attitudes and behaviour towards Travellers in the local and wider community were recognised and acknowledged by primary school headteachers and TES staff. The issue of racism and race awareness generally was not acknowledged as widely amongst secondary school teachers. The vast majority of students (almost 80 per cent) said that they had encountered racist name-calling or some form of bullying in secondary school. In almost two thirds of cases, this was not reported to teachers because students had little faith in this method of redress. Some students felt that teachers would not treat their allegations seriously or effectively, whilst others believed that reporting would lead to further victimisation. The Traveller students' responses included physical or verbal retaliation, which often came to the attention of staff, and almost half the students had been reprimanded or punished at least once including exclusion), for physical acts that were, according to the students, responses to name-calling or bullying behaviour. Racial incidents were sometimes a catalyst for withdrawal. More than a third of the students believed that certain teachers harboured and sometimes conveyed racist attitudes towards them.

Many of the students were the only Travellers in their Year 6 class. Three of the children were the only Travellers in their primary school and this minority status increased at secondary school. There were perceived advantages and disadvantages in this minority position. Students said they valued (or would value) social support from

Traveller peers but were conscious that stereotyped attitudes could result in scapegoating. Students who had older brothers or sisters whose experiences at secondary school were negative were more likely to follow suit and leave early. Conversely, students with older siblings who had positive experiences of secondary school and who stayed on until Year 11 were more likely to repeat the pattern. Students who were the first in their families to transfer were just as likely to stay on as they were to leave.

Students adopted a range of strategies to cope with their minority status in secondary school. Four of the girls were found to hide, mask or deny their cultural and ethnic identity at secondary school. Several others said that their siblings, cousins or acquaintances also adopted this tactic. This strategy, known as 'passing' is said to be used for self-protection in the context of co-existing within a pre-dominantly hostile and prejudiced majority culture (Hancock, 1997). Six other students were guarded about their heritage culture and only disclosed details of their background to close friends. Other students said that their ethnicity was obvious to those at school because of their family connections, accent or name.

More than half of the students who successfully completed Key Stage 3 (eleven) were open about their identity and made no attempt to hide or deny their background or cultural and linguistic heritage. Furthermore, eight of these students showed strong affiliations with majority culture, as well as the Traveller culture because they mixed with peers from both groups in and out of school and played an active part in school life, including extra-curricular activities. There was also an apparent link between those students who took no part in such activity and early drop-out. Most of the students who said they took no part, left school before the end of Key Stage 3. This apparent 'sense of belonging' to two cultures, without compromising one's own sense of cultural and familial identity, reflects a secure sense of cultural identity and is a life position usually referred to as biculturalism or alternation (Berry et al, 1986). However, even those students who were open about their cultural identity were wary about the idea of having their culture celebrated or promoted in school. Almost all the students said that, although they thought teachers and students had a limited awareness of Traveller culture, they did not want them to know anything else. Two students and one TES teacher described how displays on Traveller culture had caused embarrassment and engendered derogatory remarks. It is important, therefore, that positive cultural messages are woven seamlessly into the curriculum, ethos and policy of schools. Inclusive schools are those which openly acknowledge the potential effects of ethnocentrism which permeate policy and practice and encourage all students to achieve without stereotyping or pathologising behaviour which is inconsistent with sanctioned dominant culture (Yeh and Drost, 2002). The Race Relations (Amendment) Act (2000) provides the obvious vehicle for such a review. However, most senior teachers who were interviewed in secondary schools suggested that the Act would have little impact on their school.

A further suggestion which may help Traveller students to maintain a firm and positive cultural identity would be to adopt the model of supplementary provision which has been targeted at other ethnic minority groups over the past twenty years or so. Extra classes, facilitated by LEAs and taught by elders, could enable young Travellers to explore their cultural and linguistic roots in a safe forum and help to allay parental fears that the cultural is being devalued, corrupted or lost.

Achievement

Despite increasing numbers of Traveller students transferring to secondary school, retention of Traveller students remains problematic. More than half of the sample had dropped out by the end of Key Stage 3, the most common time of withdrawal being during Year 8. More than half of the students who dropped out of school attended large schools (over 1000 students), where performance in Key Stage 3 SATs and GCSE exceeded the local and national average (DfES, 2002). More than three-quarters of the students who dropped out had attendance issues at some stage during Key Stage 3, and those with the worst attendance were more likely to drop out early. Responsibility for monitoring and following up non-attendance was not always clearly defined. Problems were also exacerbated because families tended to move away, either temporarily or permanently, or they sent students to live with relatives. This made it difficult for schools and TESs to follow-up or ascertain the whereabouts of students, who then slipped through the system. Interviewee data show a link between regular attendance and secure peer relationships in school. This suggests that schools should take into account students' peer preferences when grouping them in classes as this can have a reassuring effect in the early days after transfer to secondary school. In addition, utilising aspects of the PSHE curriculum and concepts of emotional literacy can also be helpful in teaching all students social and interpersonal skills.

The study found evidence of underachievement by Traveller students in Key Stage 2 and Key Stage 3. The collection of national standardised attainment test (SATs) results revealed a spread of attainment in relation to National Curriculum core subjects at the end of Key Stage 2 (see Appendix 3). The average level of achievement for maths and English was Level 3 and for science it was Level 4. A quarter (eleven) of the sample achieved national age-related expectations (Level 4 or above) in English, just over a quarter were functioning at this level in maths and over a third attained this level in science. In contrast, nationally, in the same year (2000) around 75 per cent of students achieved Level 4 in all subjects. These comparisons reflect what Ofsted (1996) described as a 'worrying number' of Traveller students leaving their primary schools at the end of Key Stage 2, with levels of attainment that were well below national age-related expectations, although underachievement in Key Stage 1 was not identified by Ofsted. Furthermore, 45 per cent of the students in this sample were found to be on the SEN register, compared to the national general estimate of one student in five.

According to DfES statistics (2003) around 70 per cent of students nationally achieved Level 5 or above in the 2003 Key Stage 3 SATs. However, out of the twenty students in the sample who completed Key Stage 3, only four (20 per cent) achieved this level in English, and seven (35 per cent) achieved it in maths and science, showing that the attainment of Traveller students in this sample was still well below national averages. For a worrying number, nearly two-thirds (13) of the sample, achievement was below nationally expected standards in English, with slightly fewer being below this level in maths (eleven) and science (ten). This level of achievement at Key Stage 3 also reflected students' low levels of achievement at Key

Stage 2. Only one student from the sample was achieving above the nationally expected standard, which was Level 7 and above.

It has already been shown that most students in the sample were operating below the expected standard at both Key Stage 2 and 3, but were standards maintained between Key Stages or did students make any progress? Did those who achieved a Level 4 in Key Stage 2 achieve at least a Level 5 or 6 in Key Stage 3, as this would show that they had maintained their levels of achievement? Overall, half the students maintained their standards of attainment in English in Key Stage 3, but nearly a third (six) of the sample underachieved in relation to their previous scores in science, and only four students added value to their Key Stage 2 achievement (in maths and science) (see Appendix 3).

Exclusion

As a group, it has been suggested that Traveller students are disproportionately excluded from school (Ofsted, 1996, DfEE, 1999). This study found that more than a quarter (twelve) of students in the sample had been excluded from school, supporting these earlier claims. Indeed, if this pattern was replicated nationally, it would place Gypsy Travellers significantly above any other ethnic minority group in terms of exclusions from school. In this study, the excluded students comprised three girls and nine boys. Half (six) of the students who were excluded had received fixed-term exclusions at primary school. One student was permanently excluded at secondary school, whilst another was described as being on her 'last chance' in Year 9. At least three of the students in the sample had been given unofficial exclusions whereby they had been sent home by the school to 'cool off' and Dean's mum said that he had been excluded: 'for three days while Ofsted were in'.

The reasons for Traveller students' exclusion are shown in Appendix 4, with the most common reasons being physical aggression towards peers and verbal abuse towards staff. Many parents and students felt that Travellers were excluded for retaliating to other students' behaviour:

> One of the boys had been calling him names so Peter retaliated with his hands and they got into a fight and the headmaster split them up. Then he put them outside the office in the

corridor and the boy was calling him some nasty, really filthy names so Peter bopped him one. So he got excluded for that for a week. But the other boy never got excluded, just Peter and he wasn't really the same after that, he just said he didn't think it was fair. I mean I can understand it from the headmaster's point of view cos they can't condone violence ... but Peter's not the type to stand there and come out with a load of nasty language so Peter just hit him. Even the headmaster said I can quite understand Peter's point of view but he did it in front of me, as I walked out. So he had to [do something about it] (Peter's mum).

Prior to this incident, Peter had experienced no behavioural problems either in primary or secondary school.

It is clear that behavioural issues and cultural expectations about appropriate behavioural responses need to be addressed within schools, and within the classroom, as well as the reasons for such behaviour. There is perhaps a need to explore reasons behind behaviour prior to exclusion.

To conclude, whilst this study has shown that positive developments are being made in terms of increasing numbers of Traveller students transferring to secondary school and being retained in Key Stage 3, a worrying number are still not being retained. Over half of this sample of relatively sedentary students had dropped out of school by the end of Key Stage 3. Furthermore, evidence from this study has shown that Traveller students are still under-achieving, are still more likely to be excluded and are still liable to encounter racism within the school context.

Appendix 1

Thematic Framework

Interview schedules were designed around the following framework. These themes were identified by the focus group in the initial stages of the project and were used in the first phase of coding for analysis using Winmax.

- Attitudes

- Achievement

- Identity

- Involvement

- Relationships

- Expectations

- Aspirations

- Practical barriers

Appendix 2

Vocational aspirations

Name	Year 6	Year 8	Year 9
Shelley	Midwife	Midwife	Midwife but travel the world first!
Parent	I want her to have a good career	I want her to do well in exams and support her ambition to be a midwife	Supports the career choice
Leanne	Dance teacher	Dancer, dance teacher or hairdresser	Dance teacher – maybe work in Spain first
Parent		I want her to do GCSEs and would love it if she went to college	
Danny	Footballer (or carpet fitter)	Footballer or carpet fitter (would prefer footballer!)	I know now I won't be a footballer but I don't fancy carpet fitting. Like drama so maybe an actor?
Parent	We aren't looking for college. He has uncles in business	He's got to be realistic and keep an open mind. Someone in the family will teach him a trade	He still dreams of being a footballer

Name	Year 6	Year 8	Year 9
Joe	Car dealer	Mechanic – learn trade from college and uncle then set up on own	Definitely want own business – car repairs
Parent	*Whatever he wants He wants his own business*	*Uncle will take him into the family business*	*Supportive of his aspirations*
Eileen	Shop worker or pub worker	I'll leave before GCSEs. Do floristry at college with friend	Hairdresser
Parent	*Just a good job I'd like her to go to college if she could*	*Hope she gets a job and doesn't marry too young*	
Gemma	Factory worker	I'll go to upper school. Do hairdressing at college	Will take GCSEs. Then train as a hairdresser
Parent	*Leave school before exams but get a good paid job*	*Supportive of hairdressing idea*	*Thinks she'll finish school but not sure whether she'll carry on with the hairdressing idea*
Louisa	At home helping or a shop or office worker	Did not transfer	
Parent	*Home helping me out*		
Crystal	Infants teacher	Hairdresser	Lawyer, aid worker, actress or writer!
Parent	*Teacher – if that's what she wants*	*Want her to complete schooling*	*Would like her to do A levels – just have an independent life*

Name	Year 6	Year 8	Year 9
Kieran	Mechanic or builder (like granddad)	I'll leave after Year 9. Be a mechanic or a bricklayer	Bricklaying course at college
Parent	*As long as he can earn a living – I'd even be happy if he worked in McDonalds*	*Wants him to complete schooling*	*Supports the bricklaying plans*
David	Will leave before exams to work with dad or have own business	Would like to go to college and learn motor mechanics	Electrician or plasterer
Parent	*Want him to have a steady job*	*Uncle wants him to join gardening business*	*Gardening, plastering or learn a trade he's interested in*
Shane	College to learn carpentry like dad	Will complete schooling. Still interested in carpentry	Not cut out for wagon building. Sometimes thinks about being a vet but not sure what do to
Parent	*Would like him to be a vet*	*Wants him to complete schooling and it would be good to keep wagon building skills alive*	*Whatever he wants*
Ben	Leave school by 14 – learning to drive and work with granddad	Am going to have a home tutor	Has a home tutor
Parent	*Roofing with dad or work with granddad (trees) or horse dealing*	*Considering education otherwise*	

Name	Year 6	Year 8	Year 9
Charlie	Get exams and go into business with brother		Probably leave after GCSEs. Maybe a roofer or a tree surgeon
Parent	*Will support him in own choice of work. Wants him to carry on in school*		*Whatever he wants to do I'm behind him. Hope he does well in exams*
Bridget	Actress – go to drama college	Lawyer or teacher	Would like to stay to 6th form. Maybe be a beautician
Parent	*She can go to a local college but she can't go away from home*	*Would like her to go to college and be an infants teacher*	*She says she wants to do health and beauty but she changes her mind a lot Will support her whatever*
Bernie		Did not transfer	
Parent	*Would like him to stay on till 16 and then have own business*		
Linda	Leave after 16 to work with horses – horse breeder		Housewife and maybe work somewhere like Burger King
Parent	*A horse breeder or vet but to be honest a Traveller girls life is set and done (married with kids)*		

Name	Year 6	Year 8	Year 9
Kimberley		Packer in factory	Packer (like sisters)
Parent	*Have a job and some independence*	*Wants her to complete her schooling*	
Becky	Home helping mum at 14 then pub work	Work with animals on a farm	Wants to be a secretary but thinks she might get excluded first
Parent	*At school unless being bullied. I'd let her go to college*	*Any job as long as she's happy*	*Surprised but pleased she stayed in school*
Marie	Stay on at school then college to study interior design	Vet / Or if not possible something with horses	Farrier
Parent	*If she wants to go to college she can*	*Worries about financing university / Any qualification would be good*	*Will support her whatever she wants*
Connor	Singer or actor	Left in Year 7	
	Something big like a doctor or teacher or something in the music business		
Ronnie	Working with dad by 14 – hawking and cutting trees	Left in Year 8	
	He'll leave at 13		

Name	Year 6	Year 8	Year 9
Nick	Working with dad by 14 *Helping his dad by 14*	Left in Year 8	
Clint	Working with dad by 14 *Working with dad at 14*	Left in Year 8	
Stephen	Working with brothers and uncles by 14 *Working with brothers at 14.*	Left in Year 8	
Sarah Jane	At home helping mam by 14 until I get married	Will be home helping mum	Left end of Year 8
Parent	*At home helping me at 14*	*At home helping me at 14. Then she'll marry and have own family*	
Louis	Working with brother at 14 or a boxer	Left in Year 7	
Parent	*Working with older brother at 14*		
Seamus	Gardening or boxer	Did not transfer	
Parent	*Working with older brother at 14*		

Name	Year 6	Year 8	Year 9
Carly	Helping mum at home by 14 then work in a shop	Left in Year 8	
Parent	*Learn to drive and get a job*	*I want them to have a better life than I had and get a normal job like in a factory*	
Helena	Nursing	Do well in GCSEs. Do hair and beauty in college	Paediatrician
Parent	*Supports aspiration*	*Get exams. As long as she's happy, its not for me to decide her future*	*I hope she goes far and does what she wants to do*
Kenny	Complete schooling and be a footballer	Complete schooling. Professional footballer	
Parent	*To finish school and get a good job – something to do with sport?*		*Want him to have a good job – unlikely to work with dad*
Hannah	Helping me mam clean up at 14	Transferred to p/t alternative education	Wants to do part time computer course at college
Parent	*Home with me by 14*		

Name	Year 6	Year 8	Year 9
Glyn	Own business – not a posh job. Tree man or roofer	College course – building	
Parent	*Learning the ways by 14*	*Part time college course to learn a trade*	Left in Year 8
Matthew	Don't know		Left in Year 9
Parent	*Working by 14 – a job with a decent wage*		
Stacey	Complete schooling and be a hairdresser	Left in Year 8	
Parent	*To be a teacher or a secretary*		
Dean	Out working with dad at 14	Transferred to special school	Will leave in Year 10 and be doing trees
Parent	*To stay on until leaving age and then work with cars or horses*		*He wants to be a blacksmith*
Chris	Horse dealing		Left in Year 9
Parent	*Working with horses at 14*		
Kizzy	Complete schooling and be a nurse or teacher	Go to college and be a social worker	A nursery teacher
Parent	*To go to college or university and make her own decisions*		*Want her to do really well and make own decisions in life*

Name	Year 6	Year 8	Year 9
Peter	Working with dad by 14	Left in Year 7	
Parent	*To complete his schooling' He'd make a good teacher.*	*Out working with the men – that's what he is doing now*	
Chelsea	Go to college – something with computers	Maybe go to college to do hair and beauty	Hairdresser
Parent	*Probably home with me at 14 but eventually get a job*	*Supports ideas of getting qualifications but will take her out of school if bullying continues*	*Chelsea can stay in school until she decides to leave. Doesn't seem to be learning much. Supports hairdressing aspiration*

No comments in relation to aspirations were collected for Billy, Ross, Ryan (all left in Year 7) or for Samantha and Shannon (who did not transfer)

Appendix 3

Traveller students' attainment at Key Stages 2 and 3

Attainment at Key Stage 2

Level	English	Maths	Science
Below 2	10	9	8
2	4	5	4
3	18	17	13
4	10	12	15
5	1	0	3
No data	1	1	1
Total	**44**	**44**	**44**

Attainment at Key Stage 3

Level	English	Maths	Science
Below 2	1 (TA)	1 (TA)	1 (TA)
3	5 (1 TA)	3 (1 TA)	6 (2 TA)
4	7 (1 TA)	7 (1 TA)	3
5	2	5	5
6	2 (1 TA)*	1	1
7	0	1	1
Absent	2	1	2
Not applicable**	1	1	1
Total	**20**	**20**	**20**

* This student attended a school where KS3 SATs papers in English were returned for re-marking.

** Student attending a special school did not participate in the tests

Attainment and progression

Level	English	Maths	Science
Standard of attainment maintained in Key Stage 3	10	11	7
Value added in Key Stage 3	0	3	3
Standard of attainment not maintained in Key Stage 3	5	2	6
No comparable data because pupil absent for tests	3	3	3
Awaiting data	1		
Not applicable*	1	1	1
Total	**20**	**20**	**20**

*   Pupil attending a special school did not participate in the tests

Appendix 4

Reasons for Traveller students' exclusion

Student	Reasons for exclusion
A female	In Year 6 a one day exclusion for aggression towards younger students
B female	In Year 9 a total of eight days exclusion for verbal abuse to staff and physical assault on students 'I hit and punched a student ... and said 'f off' to a dinner lady'.
C female	A number of exclusions at primary school for aggressive behaviour towards peers and swearing at teachers In Year 7 a number of two-day exclusions for aggression towards peers (a response to bullying).
D male	In Year 6 for 'an accumulation of incidents' In Year 8: three days exclusion for 'defiance', two days for an assault on a student, 15 days for 'loss of control involving assault on students and staff', and another 15-day exclusion for 'defiance of all requirements – verbal abuse of students and staff'. Permanently excluded in Year 9 for physical aggression towards peers and staff.
E male	In Year 6 for behaviour A number of short-term exclusions in Years 7 and 8 In Year 9 an 11-day exclusion for physical aggression towards peers and verbal aggression towards staff.
F male	In Year 8 a one day exclusion for setting off the fire alarm

G male   End of Year 7 for a week retaliating to name calling.

H male Primary – permanently excluded (accused teacher of assault and dad assaulted headteacher)

Year 7 excluded for a couple of days for 'chewing gum'.

I male   Year 7 excluded whilst Ofsted were in (TES complained).

Year 9 excluded from school transport for refusing to wear seatbelt and throwing things out of the window.

J male   Secondary – several temporary unofficial exclusions when sent home to 'cool off'.

K male   Year 8 excluded one day (reason not given).

L male   In Year 6 a two-day exclusion for fighting in the classroom.

M male   Year 8 three-day exclusion for 'rude, unacceptable behaviour'.

Bibliography

Acton, T.A. (1974) *Gypsy Politics and Social Change.* London: Routledge and Kegan Paul.

Acton, T.A., Marselos, V. and Szego, L. 'The Development of Literary Dialects of Romanes, and the prospects for an international standard dialect'. In: Acton, T and Dalphinis, M. (2000) *Language, Blacks and Gypsies: languages without a written tradition and their role in education.* London: Whiting and Birch Ltd.

Acton, T.A. and Kenrick, D. (1985) *The Education of Gypsy/Traveller Children in Great Britain and Northern Ireland.* Report prepared for the Commission of the EEC.

Adams, B., Okely, J., Morgan, D. and Smith, D. (1975) *Gypsies and Government Policy in England.* London: Heinemann.

Andereck, M.E. (1992) *Ethnic Awareness and the School.* New York: Sage

Atkinson, M., Halsey, K., Wilkin, A. And Kinder, K. (2000) *Raising Attendance.* Slough: NFER.

Audit Commission. (1996) *Misspent Youth.* London: Audit Commission

Batsche, G. M. and Knoff, H. M. (1994) 'Bullies and their victims: Understanding a pervasive problem in the schools', *Psychology Review,* 23, 2, 165-174.

Bedford, S and Rawcliffe, B. (1999) *Porraimos: A brief introduction to Gypsies and the holocaust.* Northamptonshire County Council.

Berry, J., Trimble, J. and Olmedo, E. (1986) 'Assessment of acculturation', In: Lonner, W. and Berry, J. (Eds). *Field methods in cross-cultural research.* Newbury Park, CA: Sage.

Bhopal, K. with Gundara, J., Jones, C. and Owen, C. (2000) *Working Towards Inclusive Education for Gypsy Traveller Pupils* (RR 238). London: DfEE.

Binchy, A. (2000) 'Shelta/Gammon in Dublin'. In Acton, T. and Dalphinis, M. (2000) *Language, Blacks and Gypsies: languages without a written tradition and their role in education.* London: Whiting and Birch Ltd.

Bronfenbrenner, U. (1979) *The Ecology of Human Development.* Cambridge: Harvard University Press.

Clay, S. (1999) Traveller Children's Schooling. Unpublished Ph.D. thesis, Cardiff, University of Wales.

Cline, T., De Abreu, G., Fihosy, C., Gray, H., Lambert, H. and Neale, J. (2002) *Minority Pupils in Mainly White Schools*. London: DfES Research Briefing Paper 365.

Connolly, P. (1998) *Racism, Gender Identities and Young Children*. London: Routledge.

Cooper, P. (Ed) (1999) *Understanding and supporting children with emotional and behavioural difficulties*. London: Jessica Kingsley.

Courthaide, M. (1993) 'The work of research and action group on Romani linguistics'. *Interface*, 9, 3-7.

Creswell, J.W. (1994) *Research Design: Qualitative and Quantitative Approaches*. London: Sage Publications.

Cross, W. (1978) 'The Thomas and Cross models of psychological nigrescence: A literature review'. *Journal of Black Psychology*, 4, 13-31.

Currie, H and Danaher, P.A. (2001) 'Government funding for English Traveller Education Support Services'. *Multicultural Teaching*, 19 (2)

Delamont, S. (1991) 'The hit list and other horror stories'. *Sociological Review*, 39, 2, p.238-259

Department for Education (1994) *School Attendance: Policy and Practice on Categorisation of Absence*. London: DFE.

Department for Education and Employment (1999) *Social Inclusion: Pupil Support* (Circular 10/99 Annex A). London: DfEE.

Department for Education and Employment (1999) *Tackling Truancy Together: A strategy document*. London: DfEE.

Department for Education and Skills (2002) *School standards performance data*. London: DfES.

Department for Education and Skills (2003) *Aiming High: Raising the Achievement of Minority Ethnic Pupils*. London: DfES.

Department of Education and Science. (1967) *Children and their Primary Schools. The Plowden Report. Central Advisory Council For Education (England)* London: HMSO.

Department of Education and Science (1985) *Education for All: the report of the committee of enquiry into the education of children from ethnic minority groups (The Swann Report)*. London: HMSO.

Department of Education and Science (1990) *The Education Reform Act 1988: Specific Grant for the Education of Travellers and Displaced Persons* (Circular 10/90 Section 210). London: DES.

Derrington, C and Thorp, S. (1990) *Racism and Travellers: School and Teachers' Responses*. Northamptonshire County Council

England and Wales Statutes (1994) *The Criminal Justice and Public order Act 1994. Part V.* London: The Stationery Office

England and Wales Statutes (2000) *Race Relations (Amendment) Act 2000. Chapter 34.* London: The Stationery Office.

Erikson, E. (1968) *Identity: Youth and crisis*. New York: Norton.

Fraenkal, J.R. And Wallen, N.E. (1990) *How to design and evaluate research in education*. New York: McGraw-Hill.

Glaser, B.G. And Strauss, A.L. (1967) *The Discovery of Grounded Theory.* Chicago: Aldane.

Gross, H. and Burdett, G. (1996) 'Coping with school transfer: predicting and using coping strategies', *Pastoral Care in Education*, 14, 3, 38-44.

Hancock, I. (1997) 'The struggle for the control of identity'. *Patrin Web Journal* 4, 4.

Hancock, I. (2000) 'Standardisation and Ethnic Defence in Emergent Non-Literate Societies: The Gypsy and Caribbean Cases'. in Acton, T. and Dalphinis, M. (Eds) *Language, Blacks and Gypsies.* London: Whiting and Birch Ltd.

Hardy, H. (1988) 'Developing links: the secondary school experience', *Management in Education*, 2, 4, 34-7.

Hawes, D. and Perez, B. (1995) *The Gypsy and the State: The ethnic cleansing of British Society.* Bristol: SAUS Publications.

HMI (1983) *The Education of Travellers' Children.* London: HMSO.

Hyman, M. (1989) *Sites for Travellers.* Runnymede.

Ivatts, A. (2003) *Roma/Gypsies in Europe: The Quintessence of Intercultural Education.* Paper delivered at the UNESCO World conference, Finland, June 2003.

Ivatts A. (1975) *Catch 22 Gypsies.* ACERT.

Jordan, E. (Ed) (1996) *Inclusive Education for Secondary Age Travellers.* Edinburgh: STEP at Moray House Institute of Education.

Jordan, E. (2001) 'From interdependence to dependence and independence: home and school learning for Traveller children'. *Childhood*, 8, 1, 57-74.

Kelly, E and Cohen, T. (1988) *Racism in Schools: New Research Evidence.* Stoke on Trent: Trentham Books

Kenrick, D. and Bakewell, S. (1995) *On the Verge: the Gypsies of England.* University of Hertfordshire Press.

Kenny, M. (1997) *The Routes of Resistance.* London: Ashgate

Kiddle, K. (1999) *Traveller Children: A Voice for Themselves.* London: Jessica Kingsley.

Kinder, K., Kendall, S., Halsey, K. and Atkinson, M. (1999) *Disaffection Talks.* Slough: NFER.

Kinder, K. and Wilkin, A. (1997) *With All Respect: Reviewing Disaffection Strategies.* Slough: NFER.

Lee, N. (1993) *Gypsies and Travellers in the United Kingdom.* In: The Education of Gypsy and Traveller Children. Report of European Conference in 1989. ACERT.

Liegeois, J-P, (1998) (2nd ed.) *School Provision for Ethnic Minorities – The Gypsy Paradigm.* Hatfield: University of Hertfordshire Press

Littlewood (1996) Gypsy Challenge. *Project Newsletter*, 2, cited by Clay (1999) Traveller Children's Schooling. Unpublished Ph.D. thesis, Cardiff, University of Wales

Lloyd G., Stead J., Jordan E. and Norris C. (1999) 'Teachers and Gypsy Travellers'. *Scottish Educational Review*, 31, 48-65.

Marcia, J. (1980) Identity in Adolescence. In J. Adelson (ed) *Handbook of Adolescent Psychology.* New York: Wiley

McCann, M., Síocháin, S.O. and Ruane, J. (eds) *Irish Travellers: Culture and Ethnicity.* Belfast: Institute of Irish Studies, Queens University of Belfast

Measor, L. and Woods, P. (1984) *Changing Schools: Pupils' Perspectives on Transfer to a Comprehensive.* Milton Keynes: Open University Press.

Merrrium, S. B. (1988) *Case Study Research in Education: A Qualitative Approach.* San Francisco: Jossey-Bass.

Messiou, K (2002) 'Marginalisation in primary schools: listening to children's voices'. *Support for Learning,* 17, 3, 117-121.

Myers, K. And Grosvenor, I. 'Policy, equality and inequality: from the past to the future'. In: Hill, D. and Cole, M. (2001) *Schooling and Equality: fact, concept and policy.* London: Kogan Page.

Nehaul, K. (1996) *The schooling of children of Caribbean heritage.* Stoke on Trent: Trentham Books.

Nicholls, G. and Gardner, J. (1999) *Pupils in Transition: Moving between Key Stages.* London: Routledge.

Nieswiadomy, R.M. (1993) 'Foundations of Nursing Research'. In: Creswell, J.W. (1994) *Research Design: Qualitative and Quantitative Approaches.* London: Sage Publications.

O'Moore, A.M., Kirkham, C. and Smith, M. (1997) 'Bullying behaviour in Irish schools: a nationwide study'. *Irish Journal of Psychology,* 18, 2, 141-69.

Office For Standards in Education (1996) *The Education of Travelling Children.* London: Ofsted.

Office For Standards in Education (1999) *Raising the Attainment of Ethnic Minority Pupils.* London: Ofsted.

Office For Standards in Education (2001) *Improving Attendance and Behaviour in Secondary Schools.* London: Ofsted.

Office For Standards in Education (2001) *Managing Support for the Attainment of Pupils from Minority Ethnic Groups.* London: Ofsted.

Olweus, D. (1993) *Bullying in schools: What we know and what we can do.* Oxford: Basil Blackwell.

Phinney, J (1989) 'Stages of ethnic identity in minority group adolescents'. *Journal of Early Adolescence,* 9, 34-49.

Phinney, J.S. 'Ethnic identity in adolescents and adults'. In: Balls (Ed), Organista, P., CHUN, K.M. And Marin, G. (1998) *Readings in Ethnic Psychology.* New York. London: Routledge.

Reiss, C. (1975) *Education of Travelling Children.* London: Macmillan.

Rose, R. and Shevlin, M. (Eds) (2003) *Encouraging Voices: Respecting the insights of young people who have been marginalised.* Dublin: NDA.

Shain, F (2003) *The Schooling and Identity of Asian Girl.* Stoke on Trent: Trentham Books

Shine, P. (1987) Traveller Education; How it is seen by teachers and Travellers. Unpublished B.Ed. dissertation, Manchester Polytechnic.

Smith, J. and Osborn, M. (2003) Interpretative phenomenological analysis. In: J. Smith (ed) *Qualitative Psychology: A practical guide to research methods.* London: Sage

Smith, P.K. and Shu, S. (2000) 'What good schools can do about bullying: Findings from a survey in English schools after a decade of research and action'. *Childhood,* 7, 193-212.

Smith, P.K. and Sharp, S. (1994) *School Bullying: Insights and Perspectives.* London: Routledge.

Tajfel, H. (1978) *The social psychology of minorities.* New York: Minority Rights Group.

Ullah, P. (1985) 'Second generation Irish youth: Identity and ethnicity'. *New Community,* 12, 310-320)

Whitney, I. and Smith, P.K. (1993) 'A Survey of the nature and extent of bully/ victim problems in junior/middle and secondary schools'. *Educational Research* 35, 3-25.

Yeh, C.J. and Drost, C. (2002) 'Bridging identities among ethnic minority youth in schools.' *ERIC Digest*, 173, (February), 1-2, Columbia University.

INDEX